Together

Luke Adam Hawker

with words by Marianne Laidlaw

Kyle Books

An Hachette UK Company
www.hachette.co.uk

First published in Great Britain in 2021 by Kyle Books,
an imprint of Octopus Publishing Group Limited
Carmelite House
50 Victoria Embankment
London EC4Y 0DZ
www.kylebooks.co.uk

ISBN: 978 0 85783 944 2

Distributed in the US by Hachette Book Group, 1290 Avenue of the Americas,
4th and 5th Floors, New York, NY 10104

Distributed in Canada by Canadian Manda Group, 664 Annette St., Toronto, Ontario,
Canada M6S 2C8

Commissioning Editor: Marianne Laidlaw
Publisher: Joanna Copestick
Assistant Editor: Florence Filose
Design: Mike Jolley
Production Manager: Caroline Alberti

A Cataloguing in Publication record for this title is available from the British Library

Printed and bound in Italy

10 9 8 7 6 5 4 3

The FSC® label means that materials used for the product have been responsibly sourced.

FSC
www.fsc.org
MIX
Paper from
responsible sources
FSC® C015829

This book is dedicated to my grandad, Brian Rupert Jewell:
forever my source of inspiration, hope and happiness.

Life can seem like a machine in constant motion.

There's no time to stop.

The clock is ticking, and there's always

somewhere we need to be.

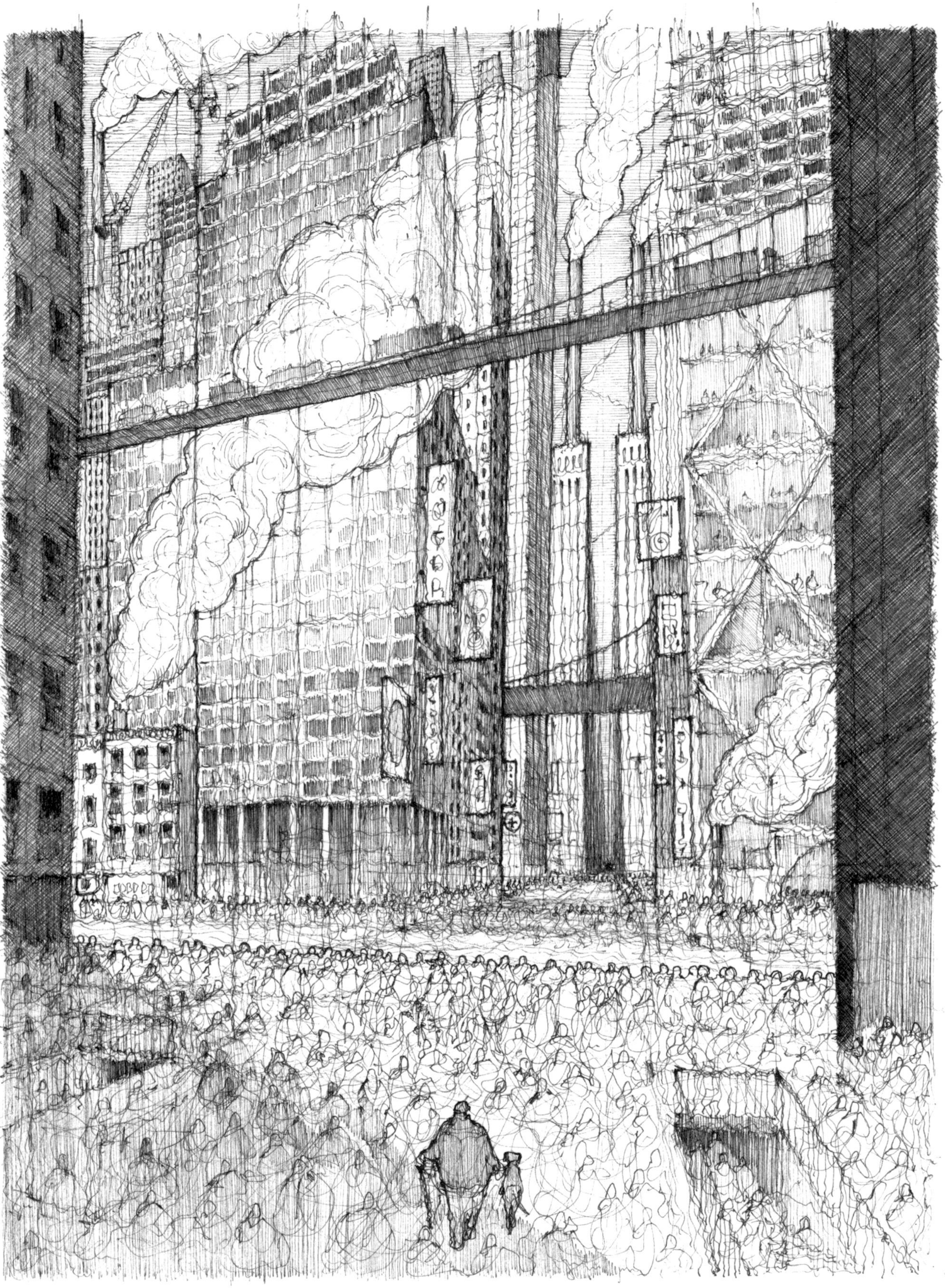

Even when we're too busy to think,
our daily rhythm sweeps us along.

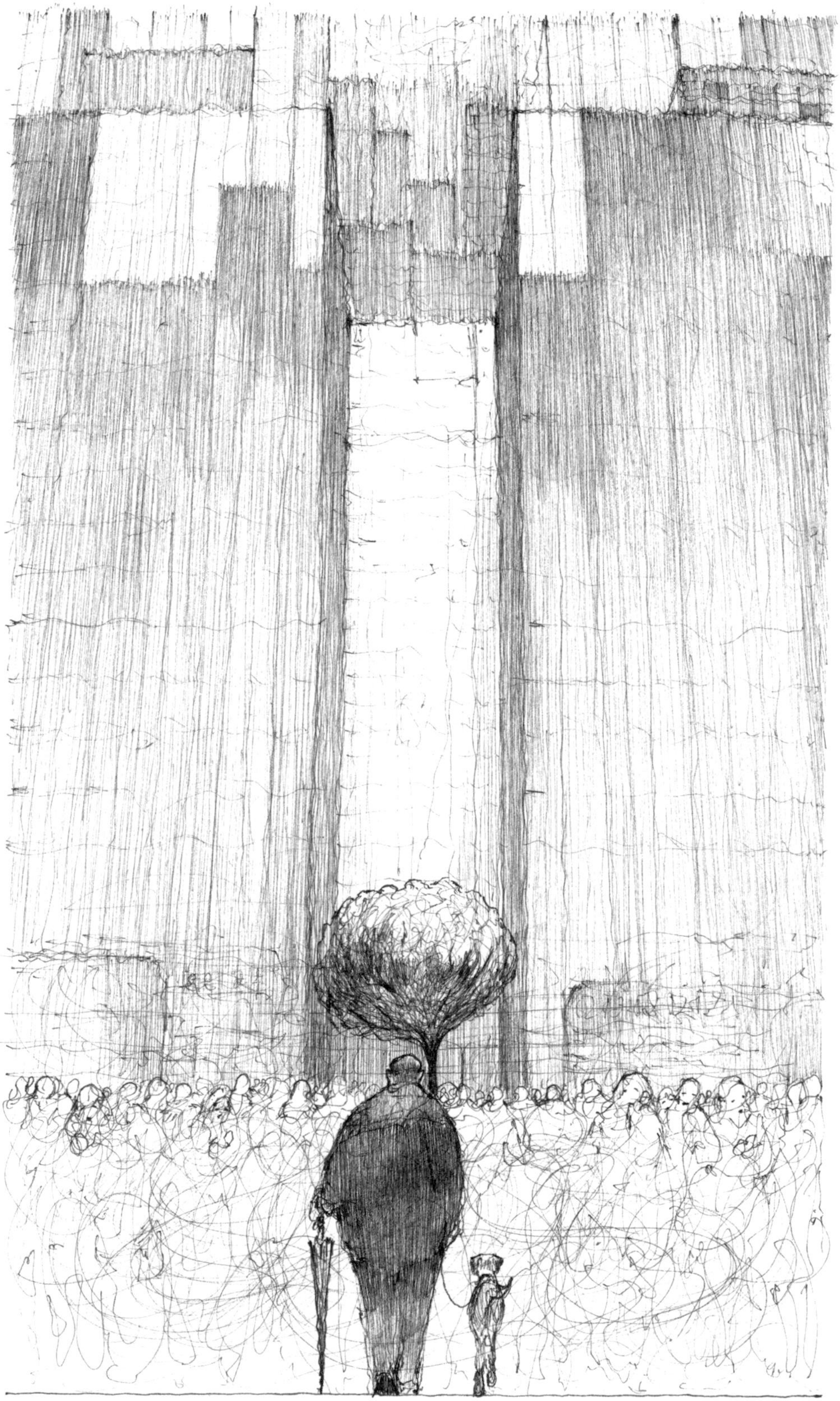

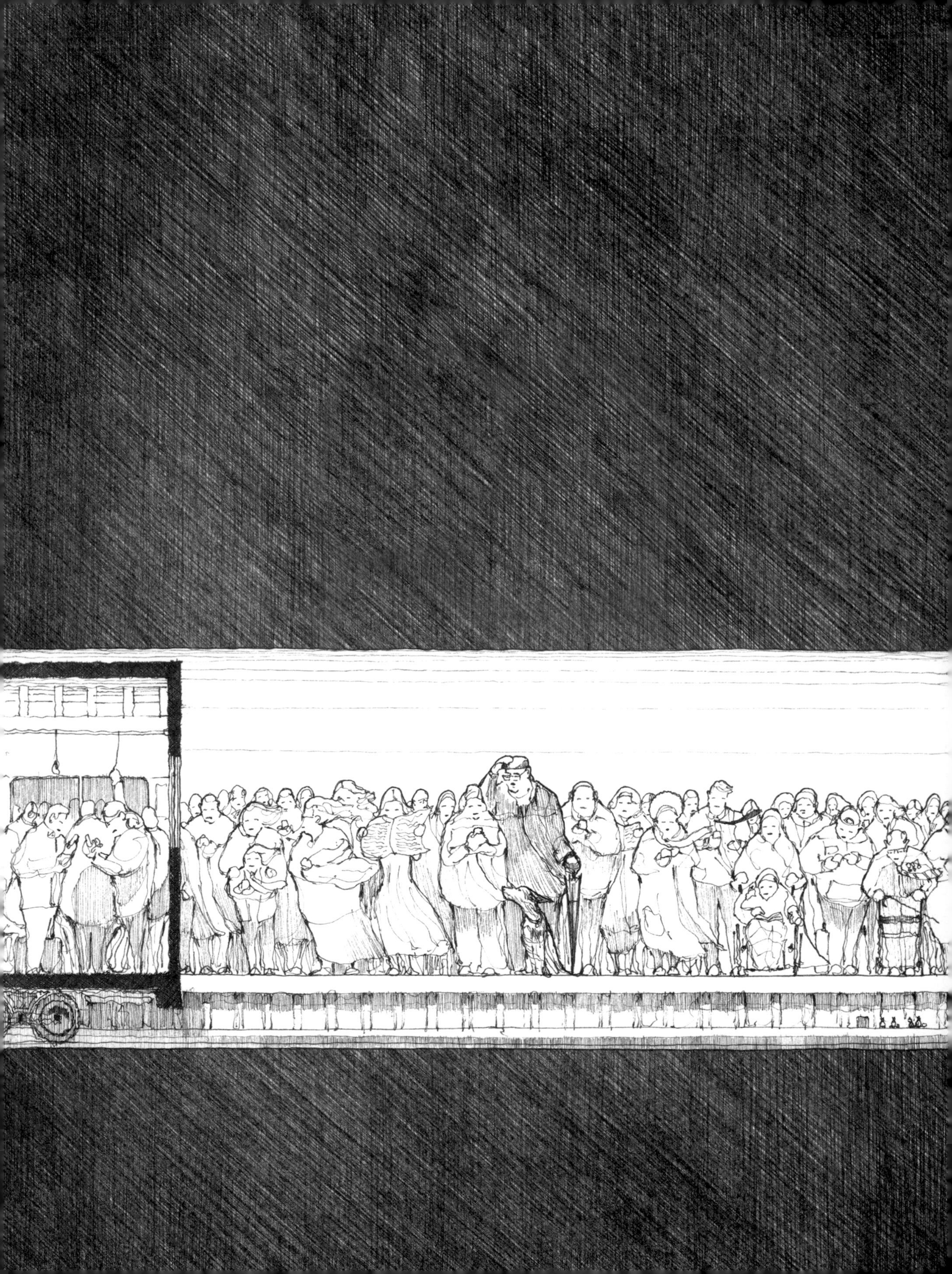

We can rush

through our days

without seeing them.

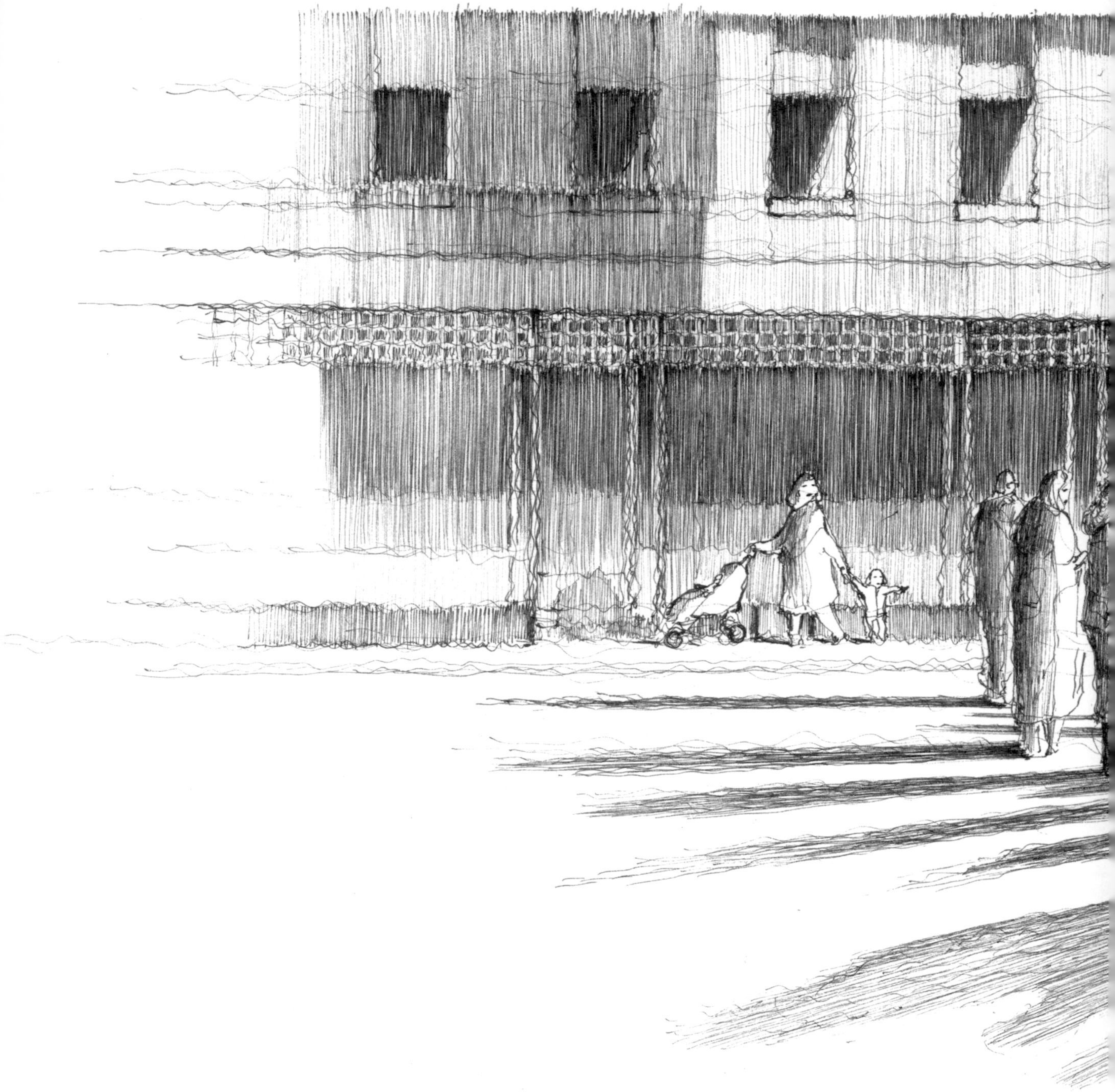

But I remember the storm that year.

An uneasy feeling was creeping amongst us.

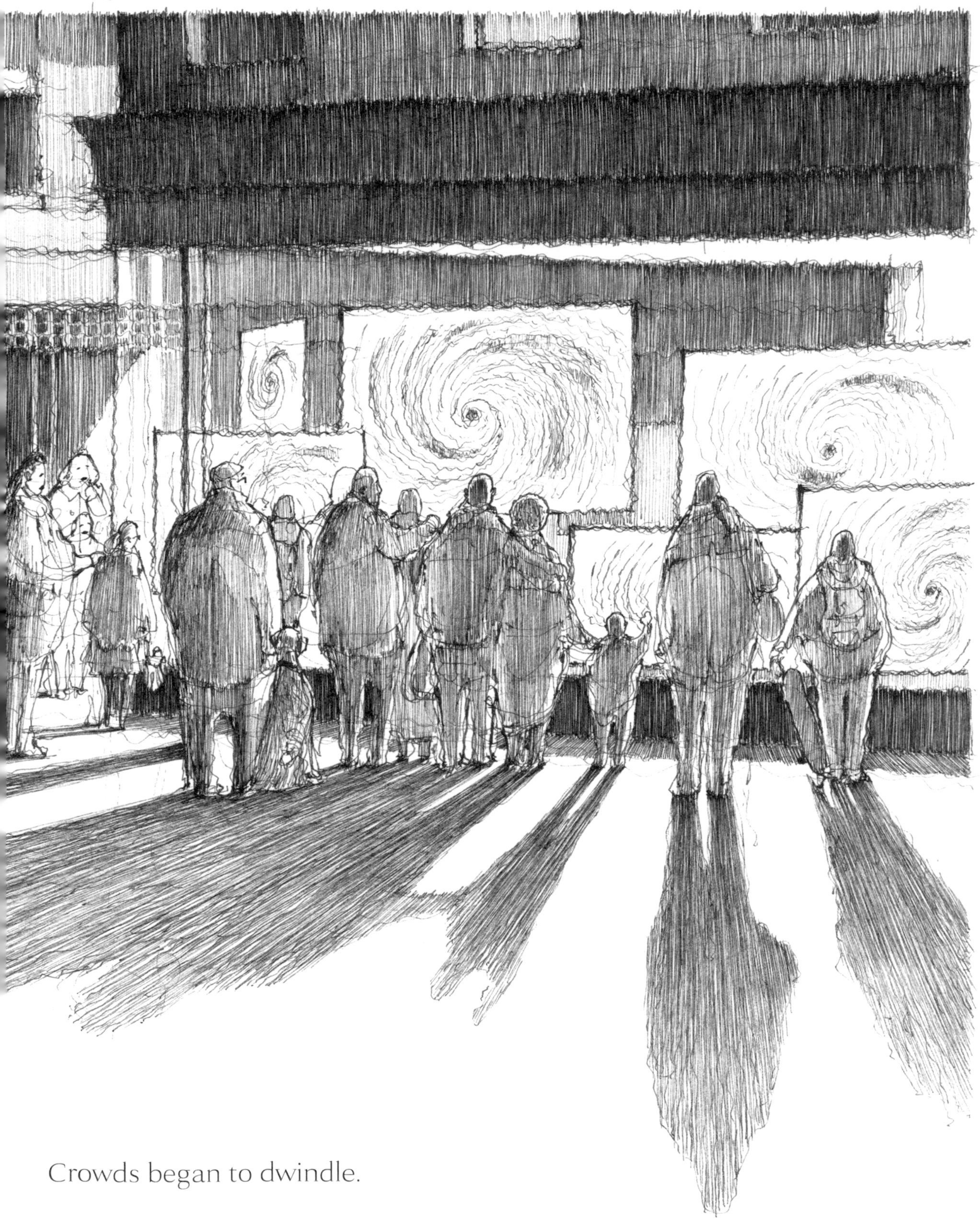

Crowds began to dwindle.

Dark clouds were looming in the distance.

We watched them gather, and we wondered...

When will it come? How long will it last?

It's hard not having all the answers.

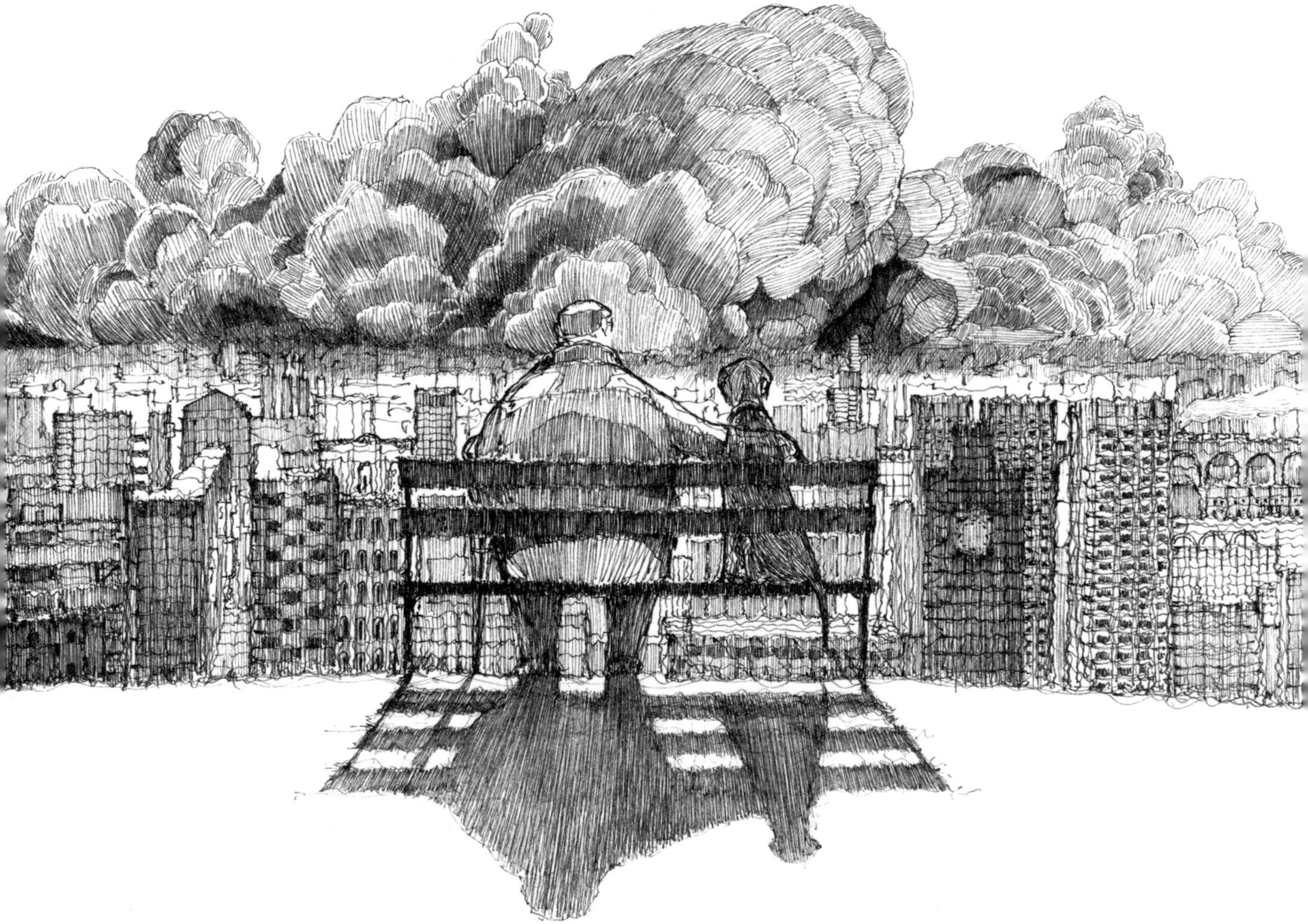

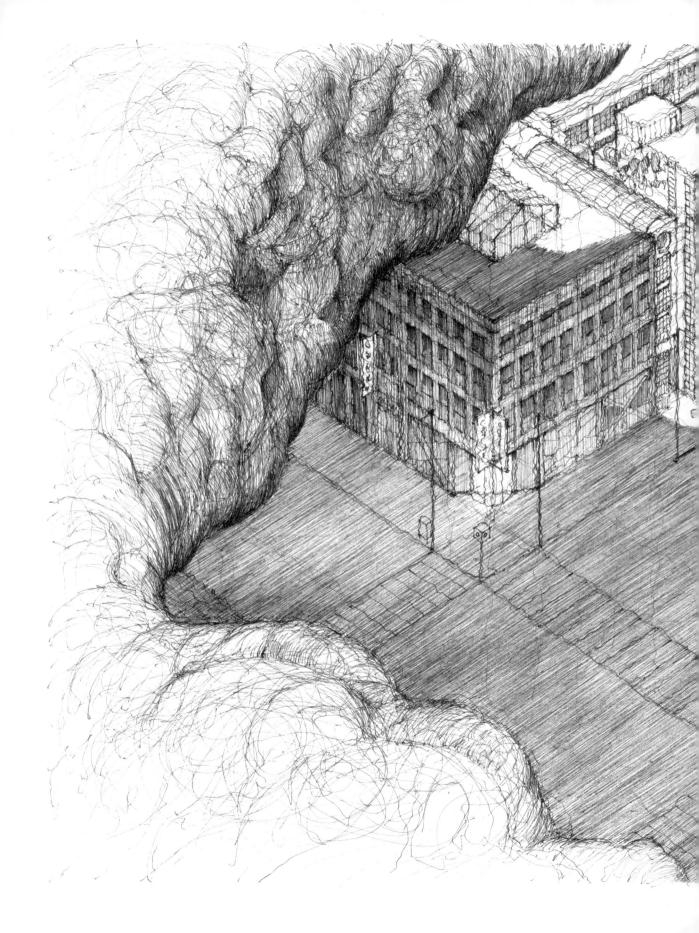

And, at once,
everything stopped.
Life's engine ground to a halt.
We could feel the weight of the
dark sky overhead.

Streets were suddenly deserted.

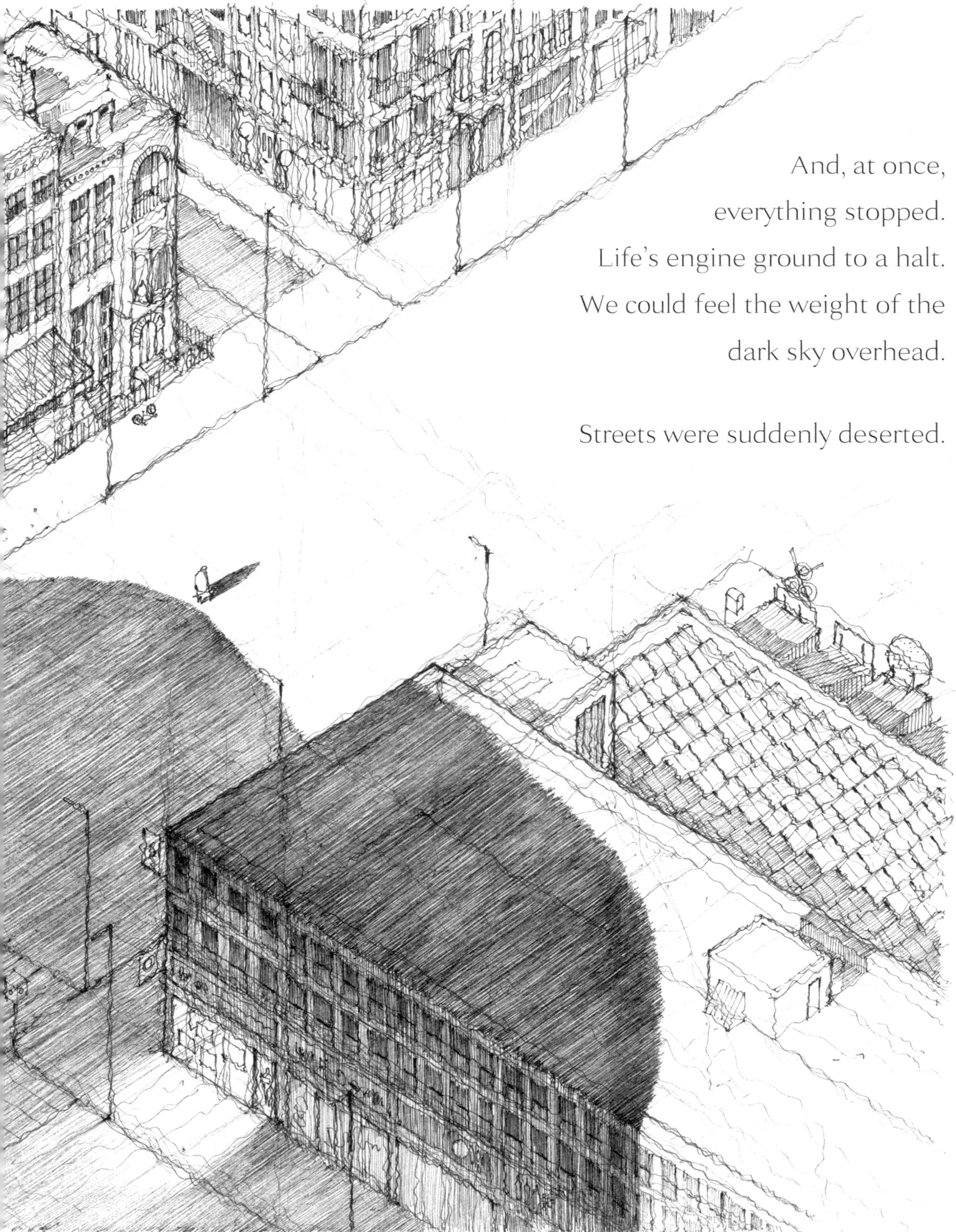

Quiet, where once there was an orchestra of noise.

The busiest of places stood empty and still.

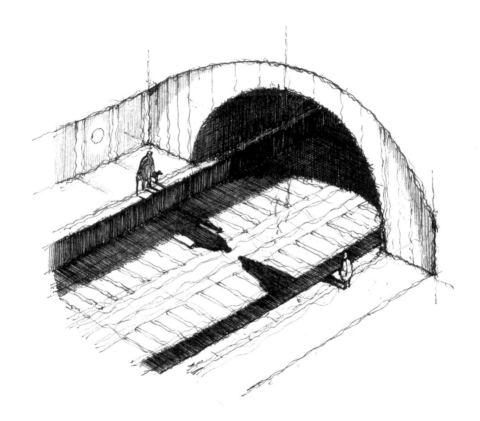

Normal things began to feel strange.

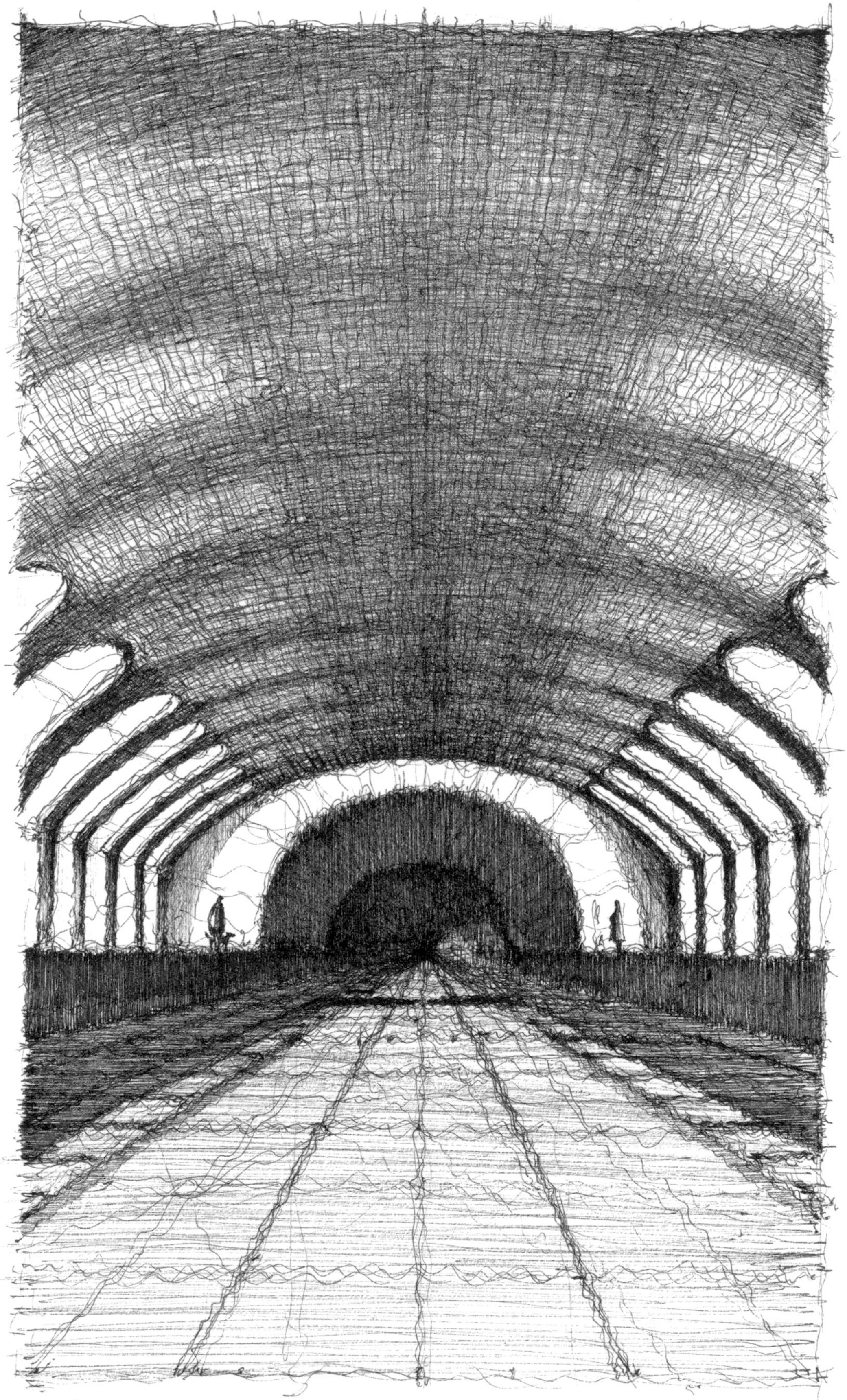

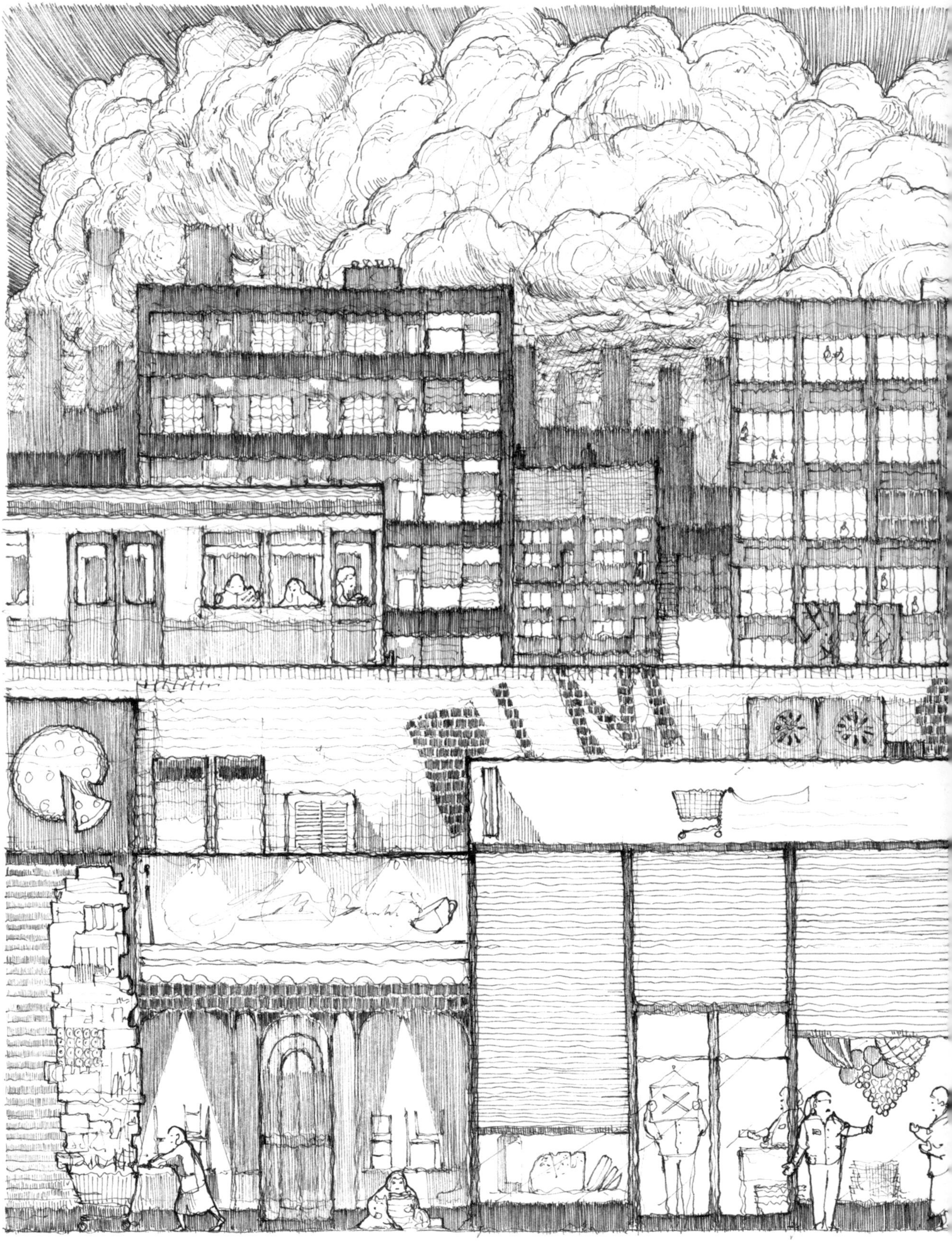

Strange things began to feel normal.

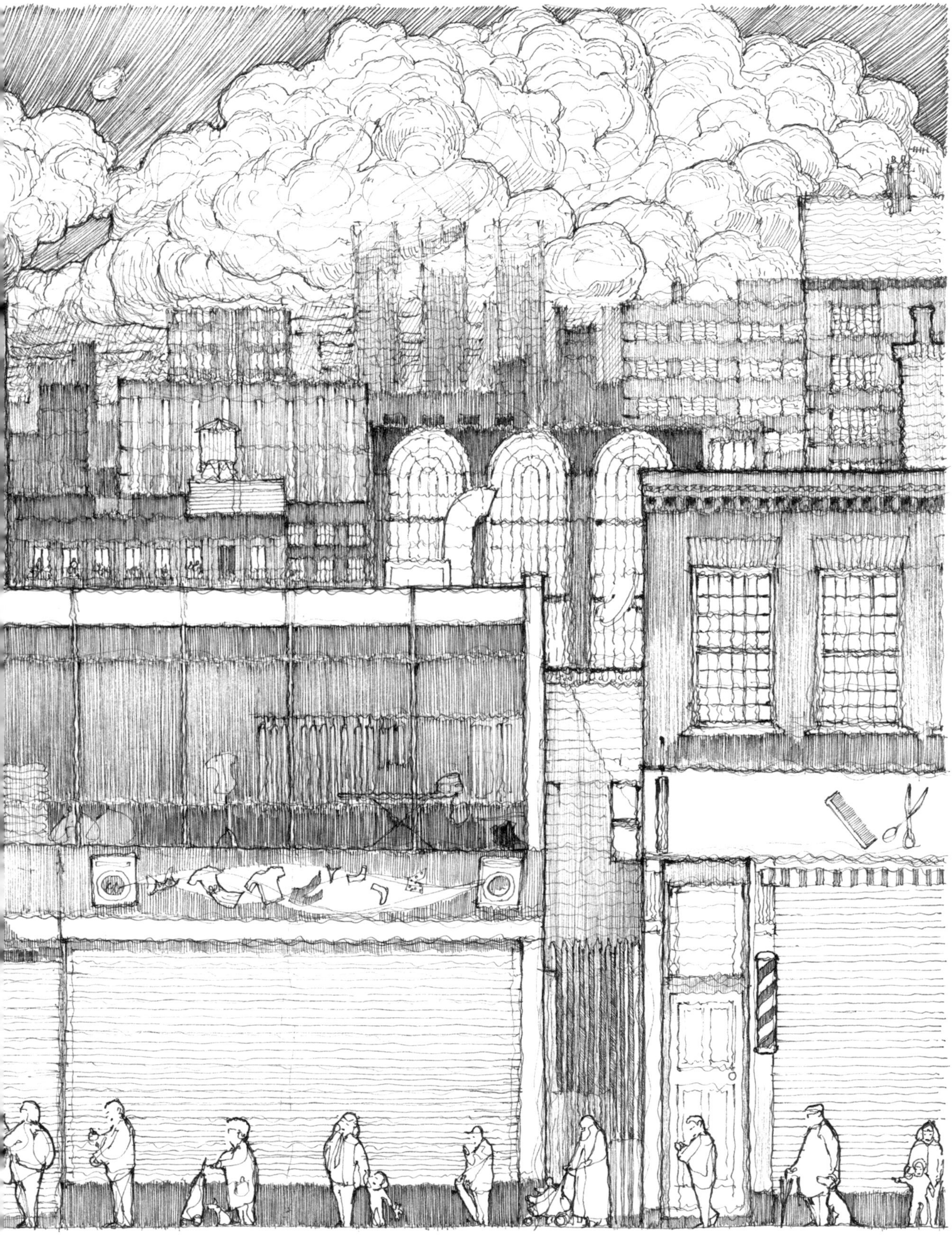

We were adrift.

.

Fear can be a funny thing; it doesn't always shine a flattering light.

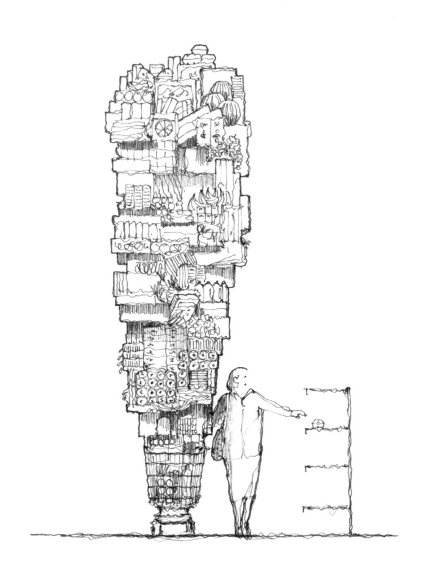

It can make us forget that others are scared too.

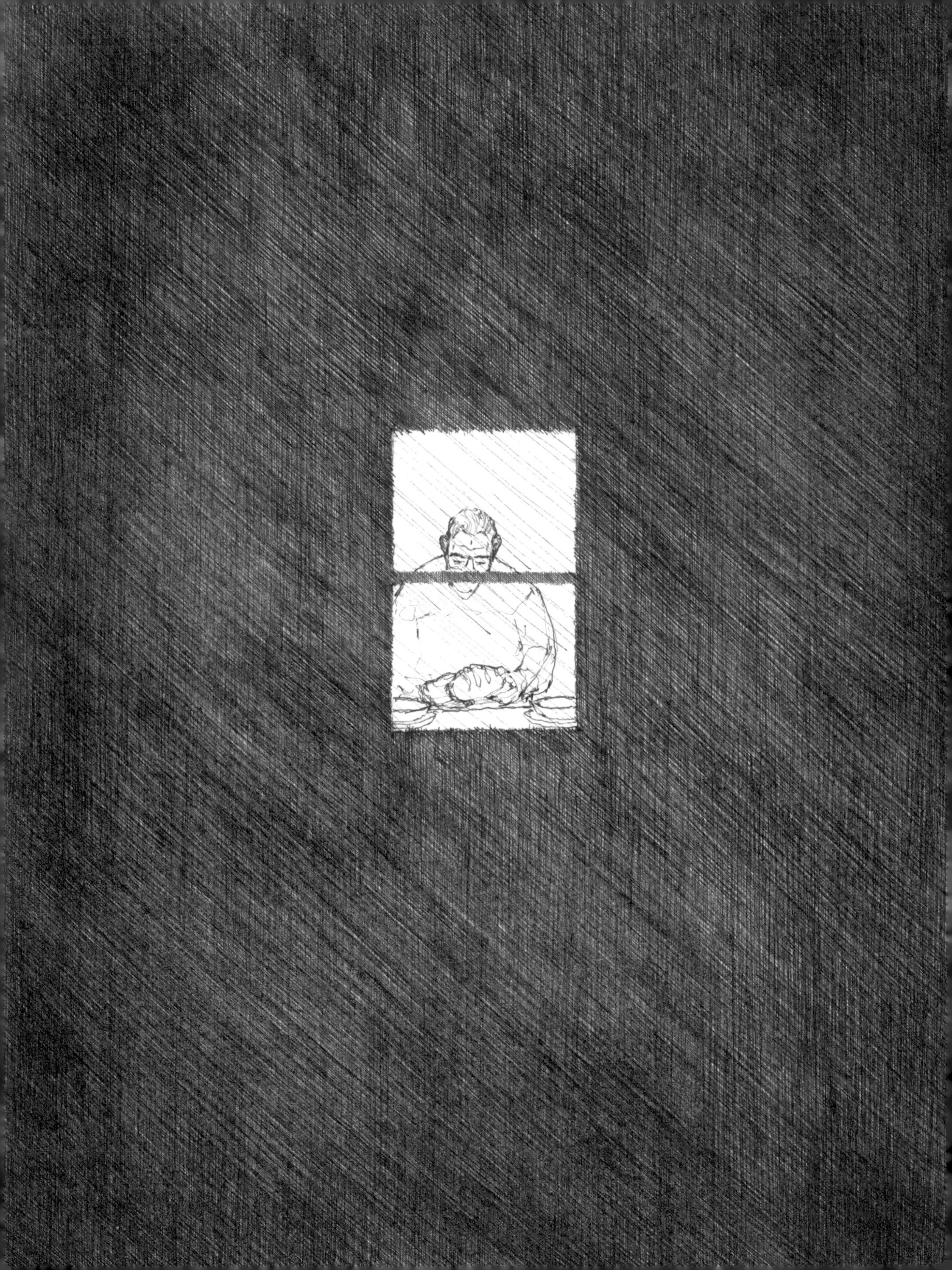

We took shelter, knowing the worst was yet to come.

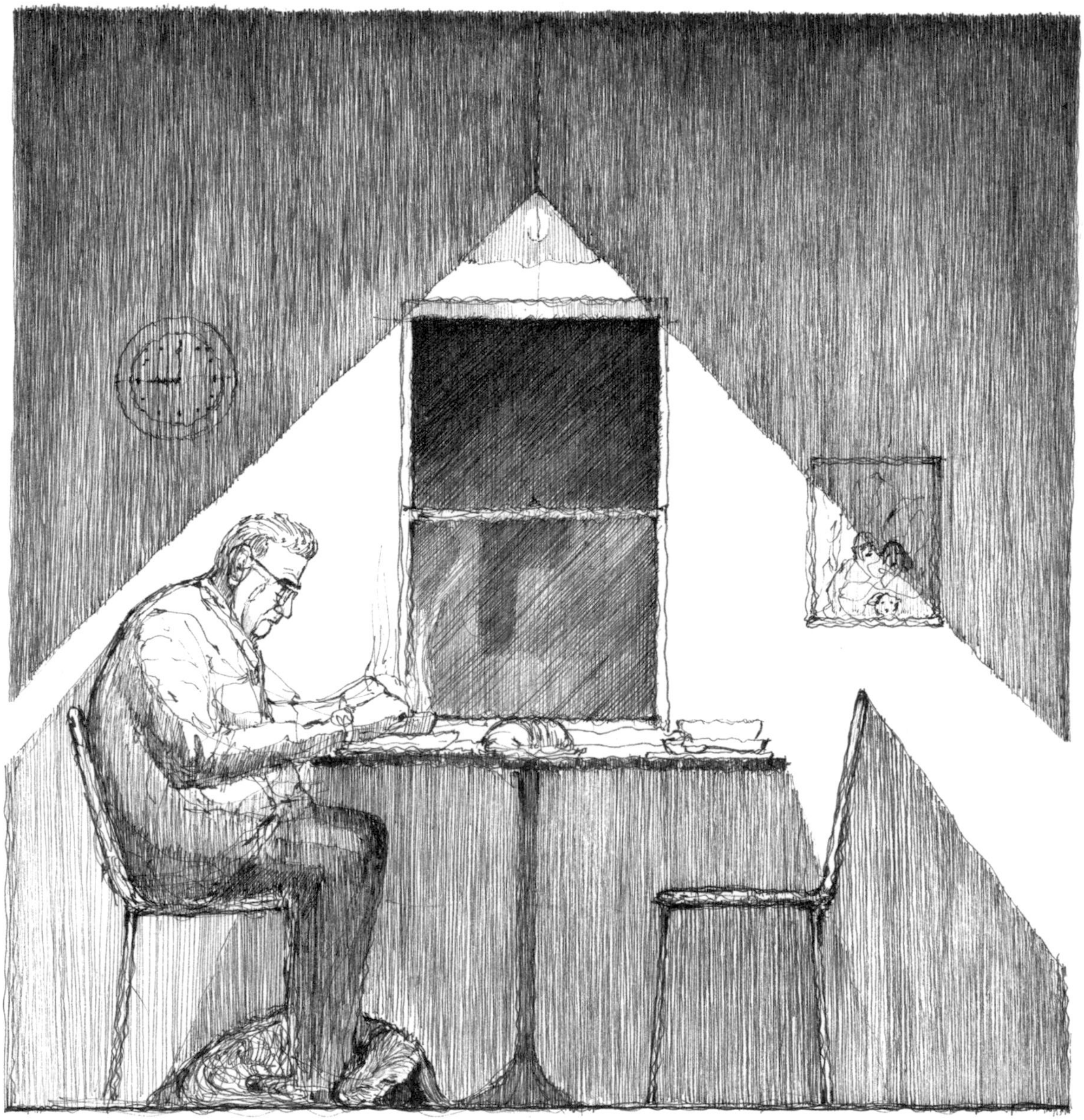

Weeks went by.

It rained and rained.

It felt like it would never end.

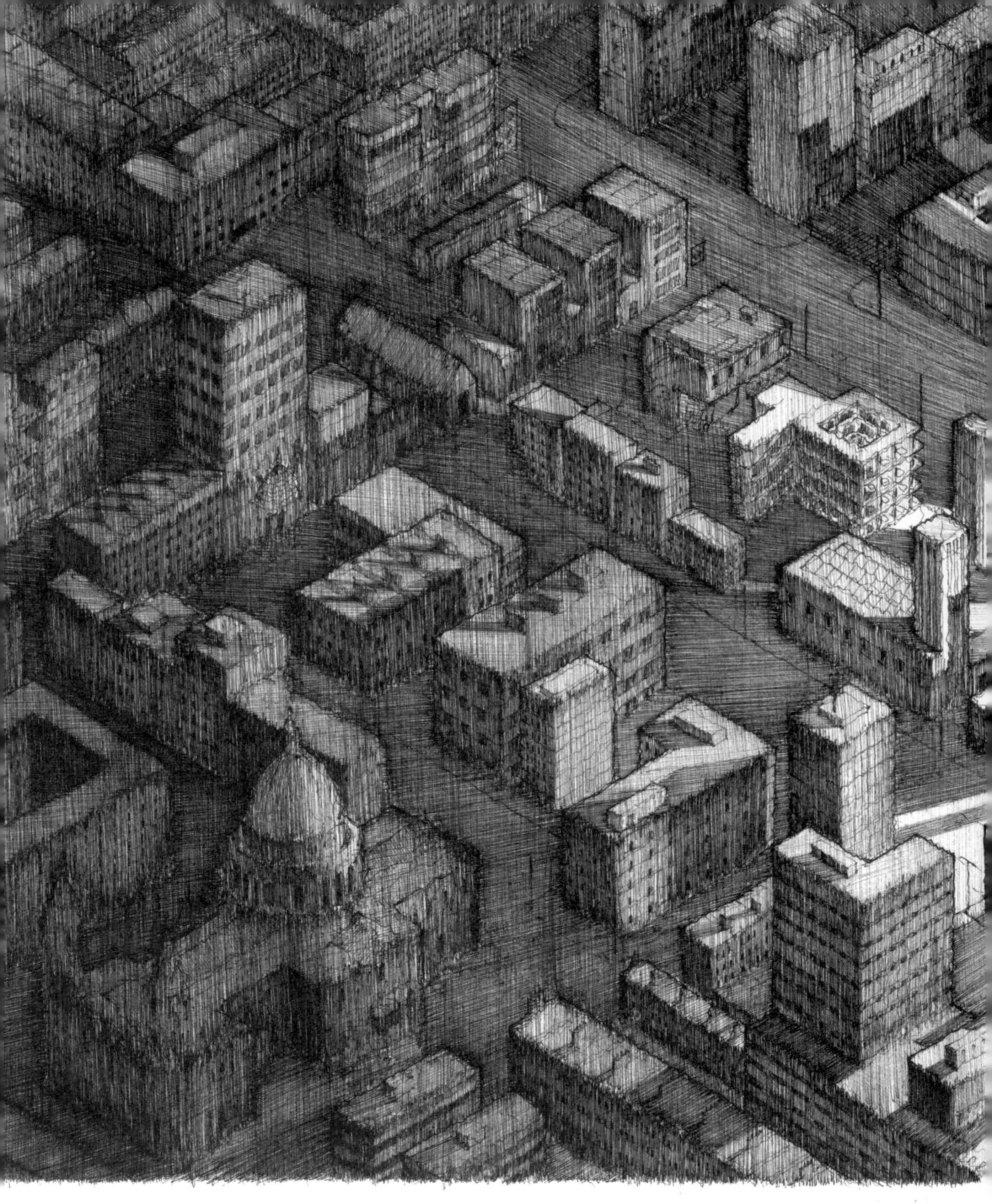

Heroes amongst us stepped forward. They held us together and put others first.

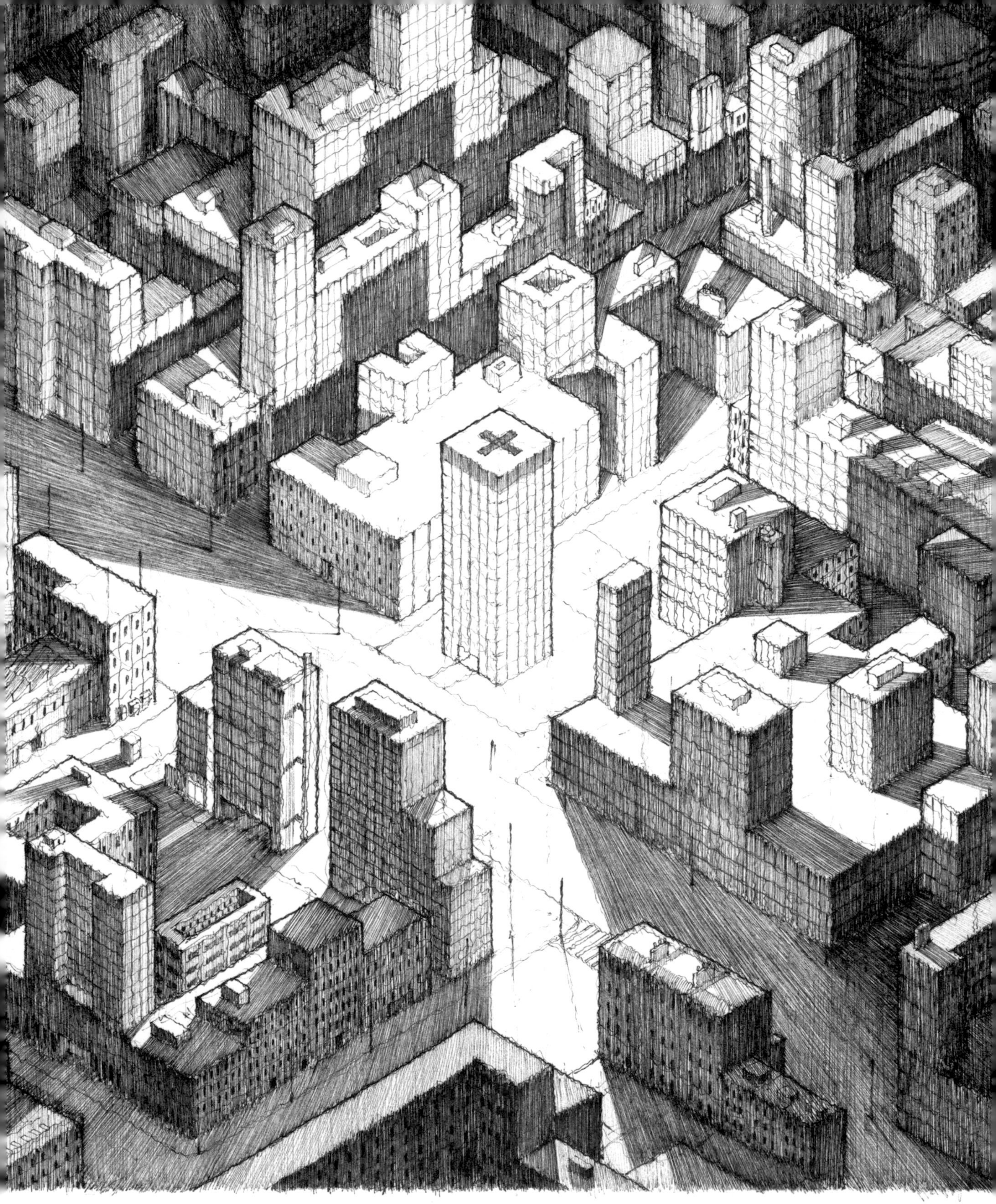

They were battling the storm in ways we could not even imagine.

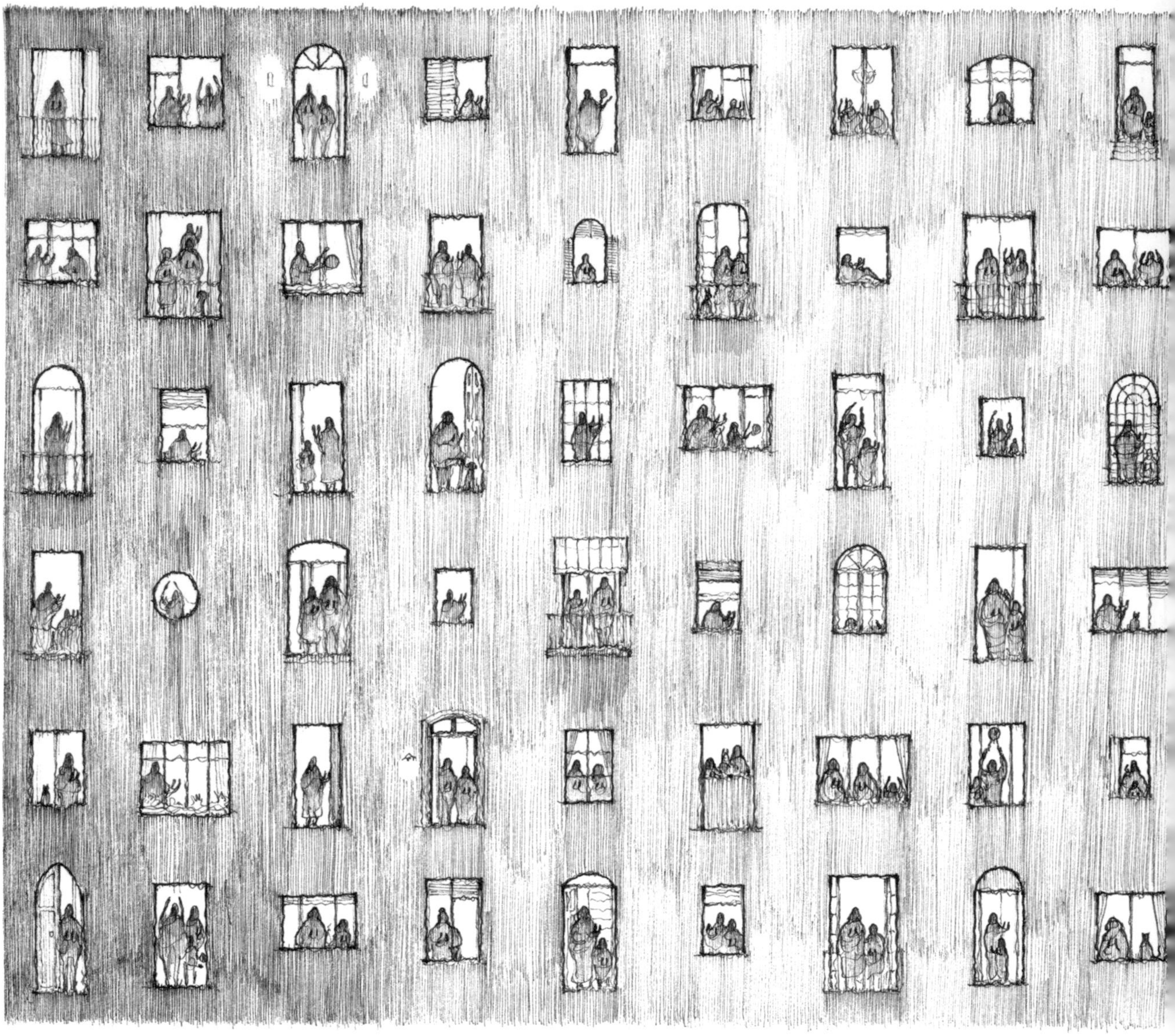

We were humbled by their courage.

They deserved our applause, and so much more...

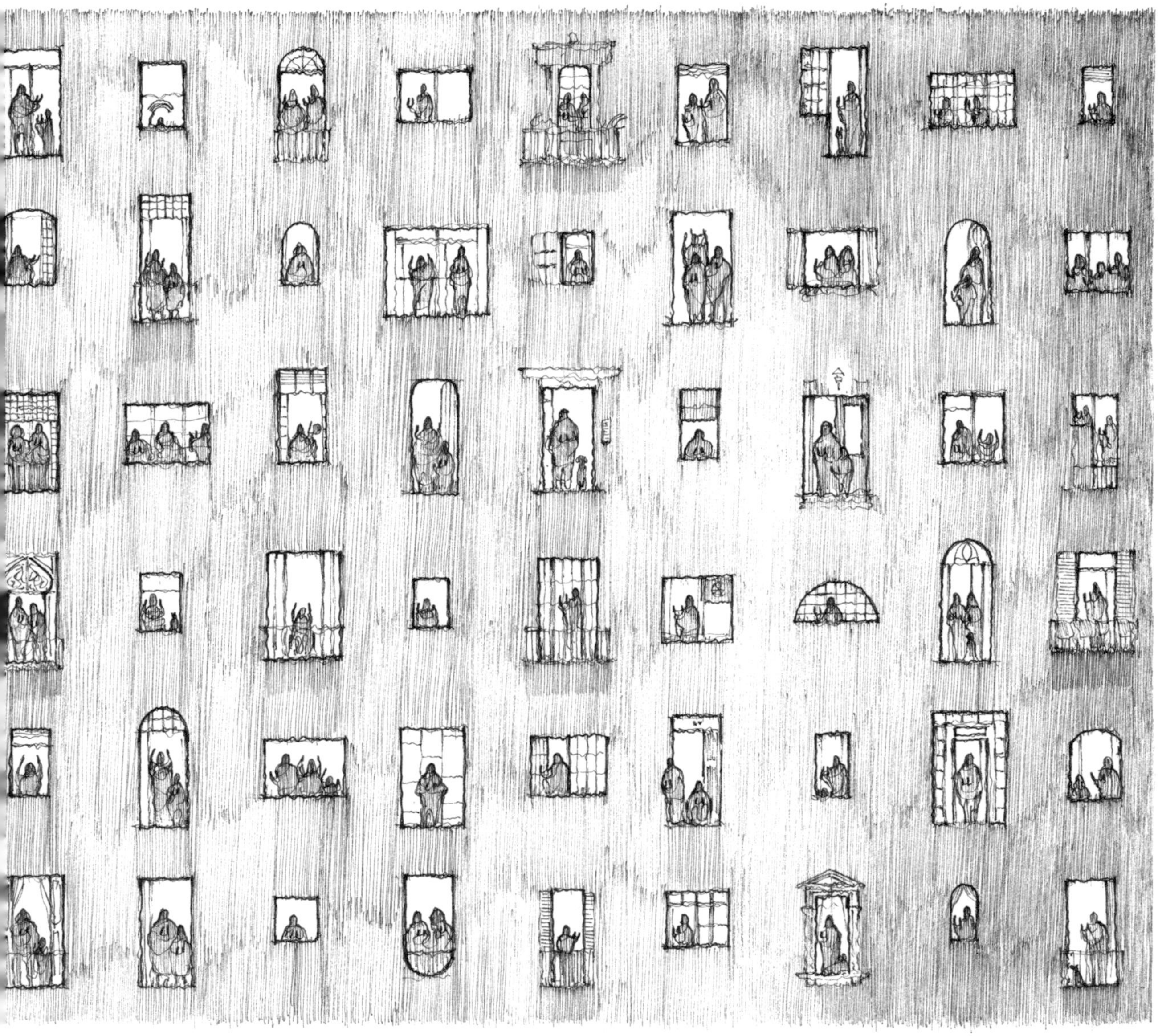

It's hard to be separated.
Worries can seem to overflow.
We felt so far apart.

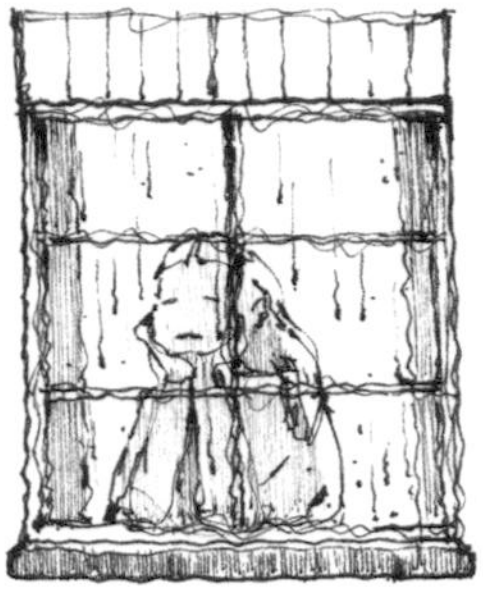

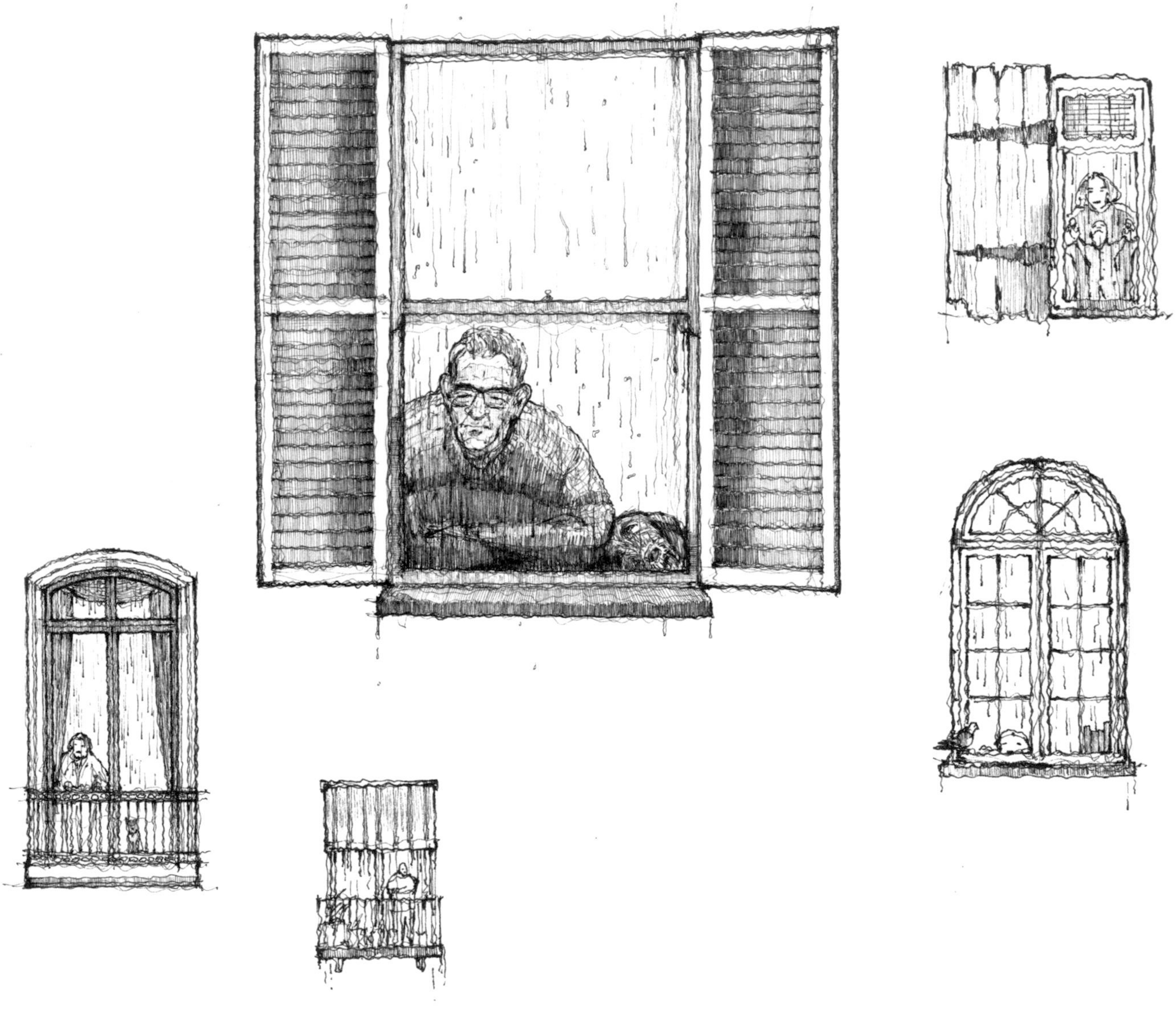

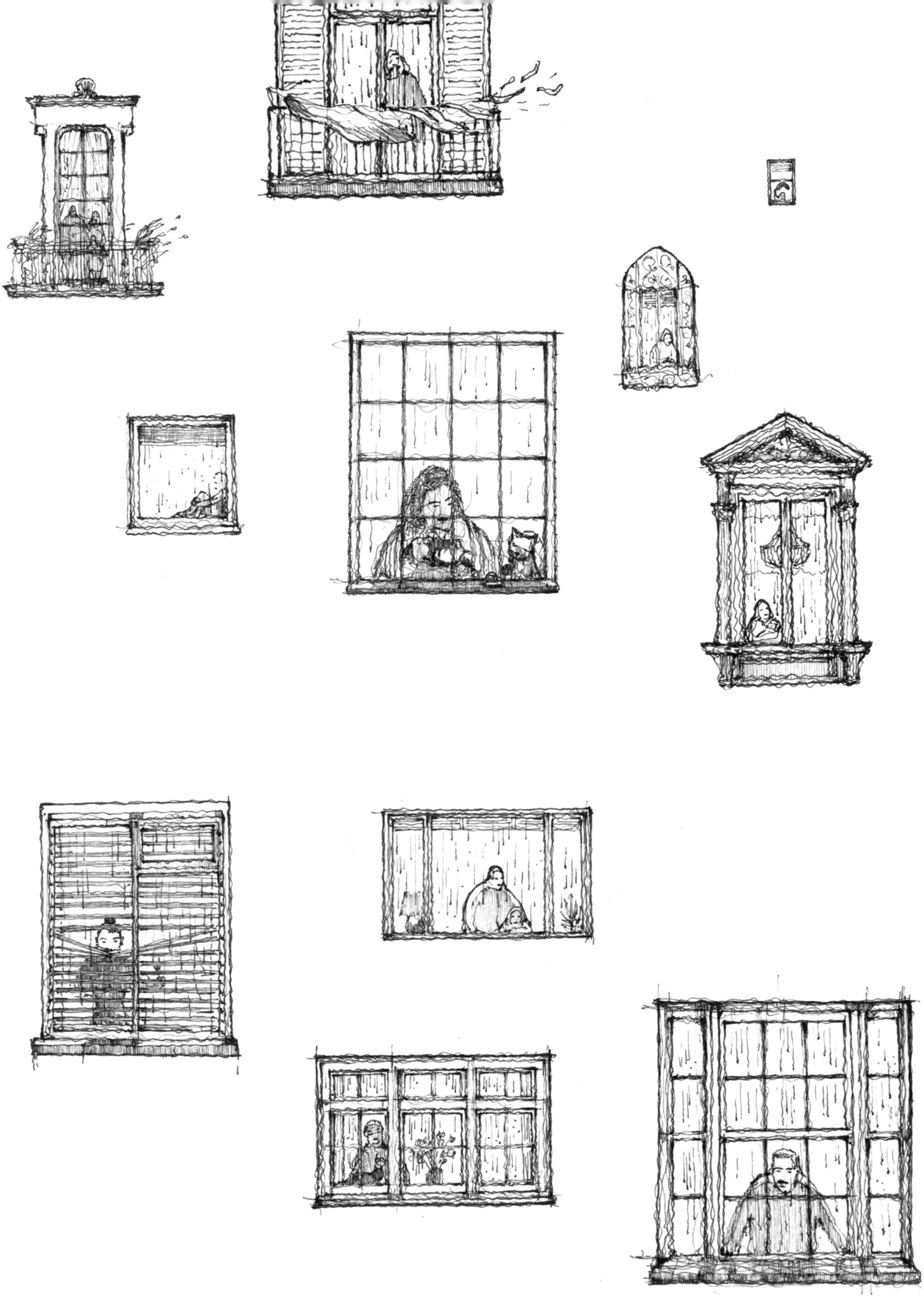

We began to understand the distances
that had been between us already...

and that loneliness can beat its drum loudest in a crowd.

But being alone doesn't have to feel lonely.

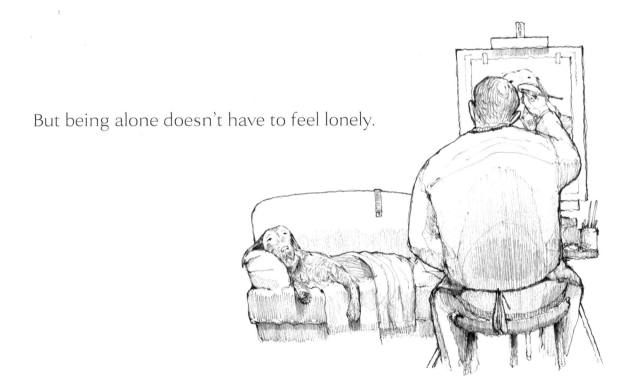

When life became smaller, we found space
to see the bigger picture.

Perhaps we were more similar than we had thought?

We were united by our separation; we were together in being apart.

We talked.

We listened.

We shared our sadness,

grief and worry.

We shared our stories

and experiences.

Hard times can help us find the best that we can be.

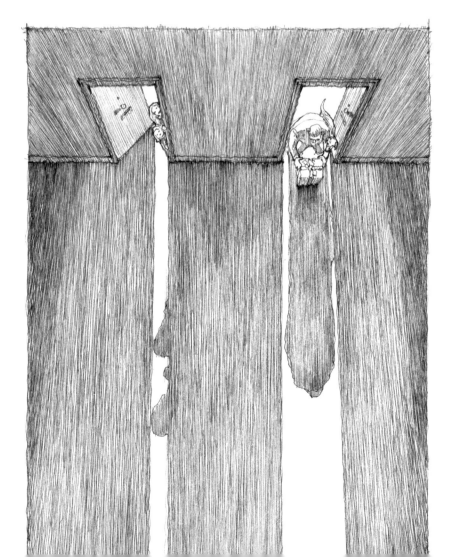

Little things can mean a lot.

Some of us found we had more time.

Time presents us with ideas to plant like seeds,

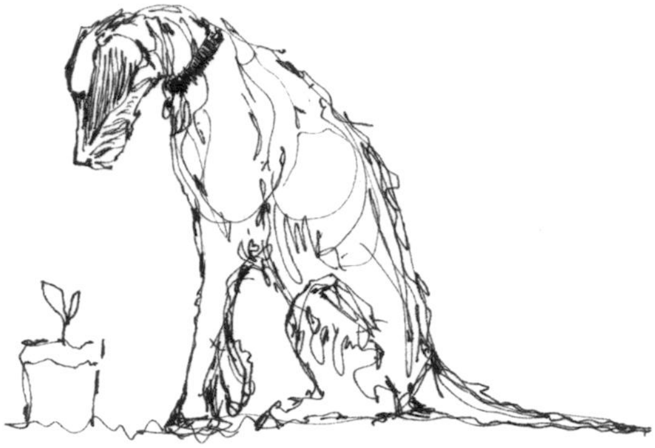

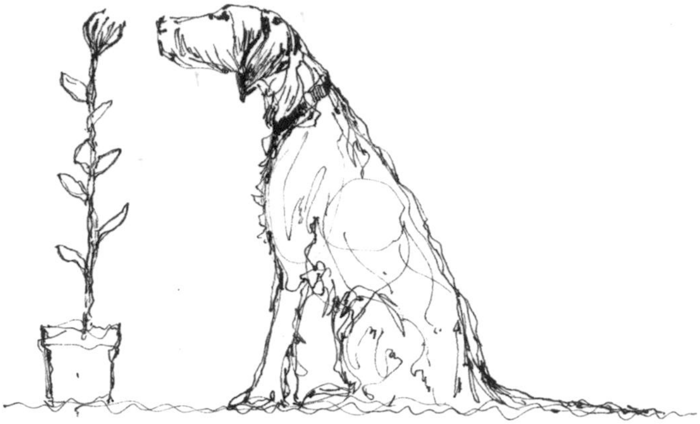

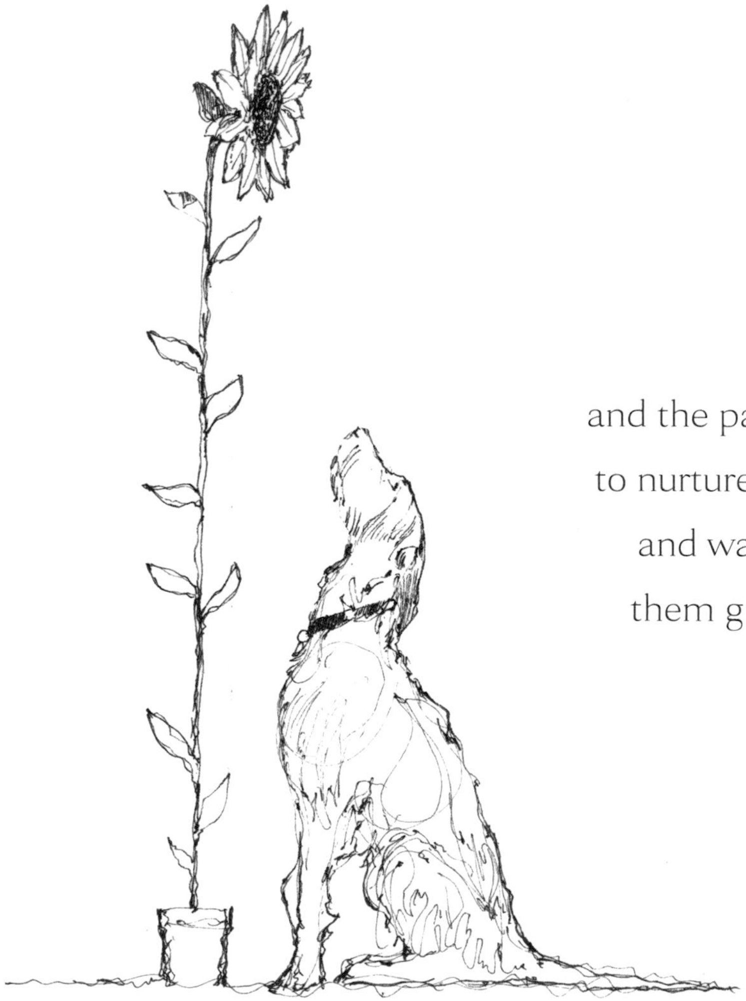

and the patience
to nurture them
and watch
them grow.

We found new ways to keep in touch.

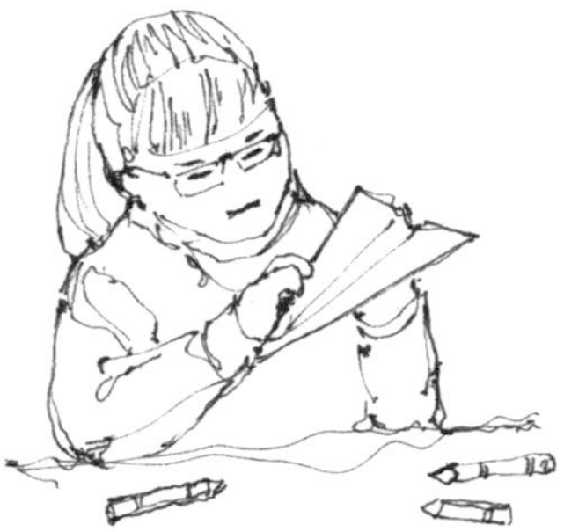

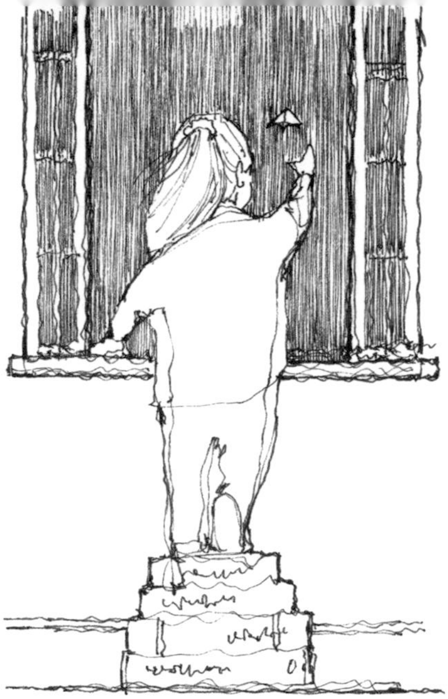

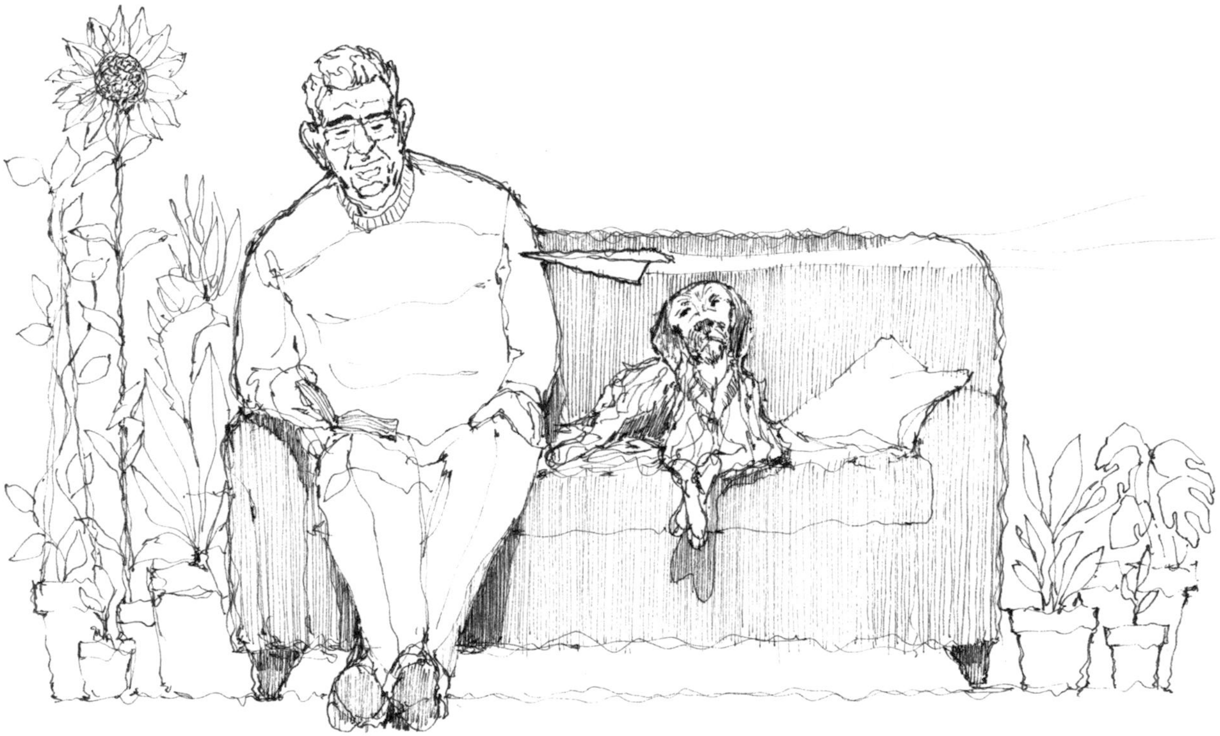

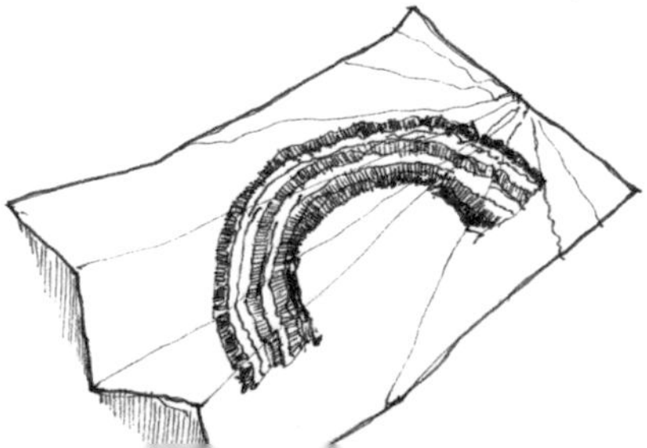

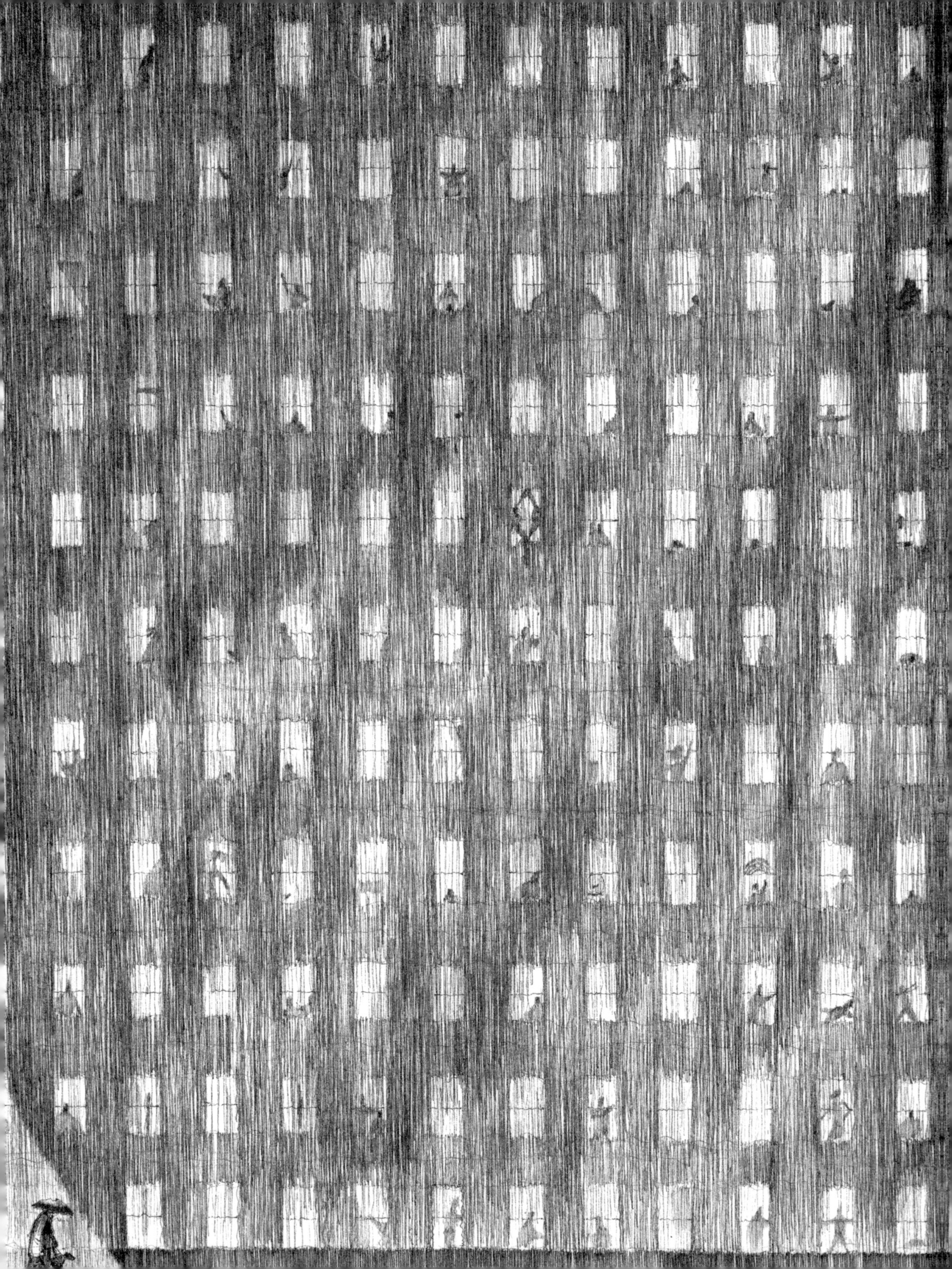

Our homes became dance halls,
classrooms, bakeries...

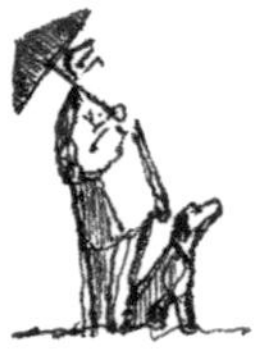

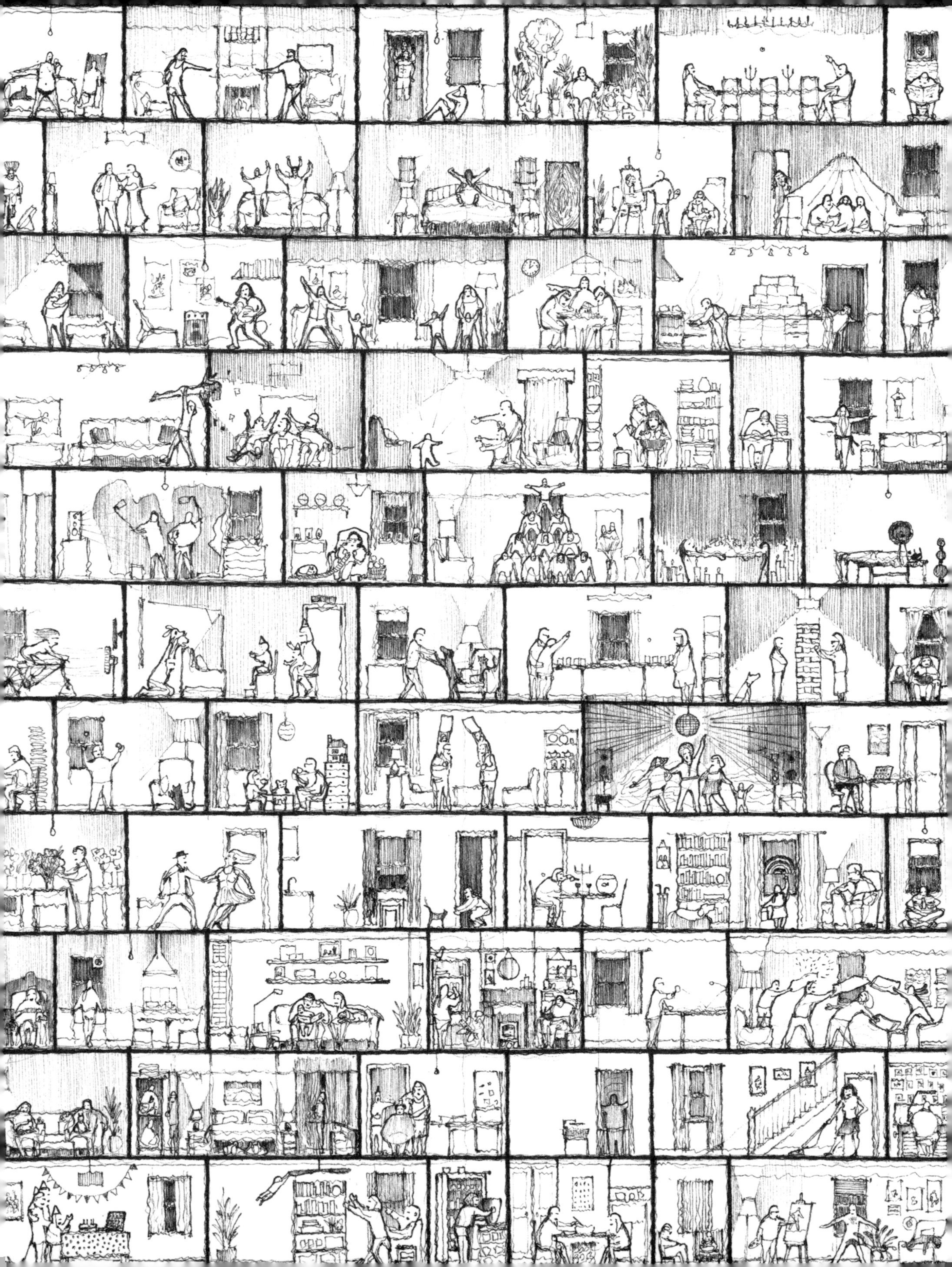

In slowing down, we woke up...

to the most important things of all.

We began to understand that the sun
was still there, rising, setting, waiting,

even when the clouds were at their darkest.

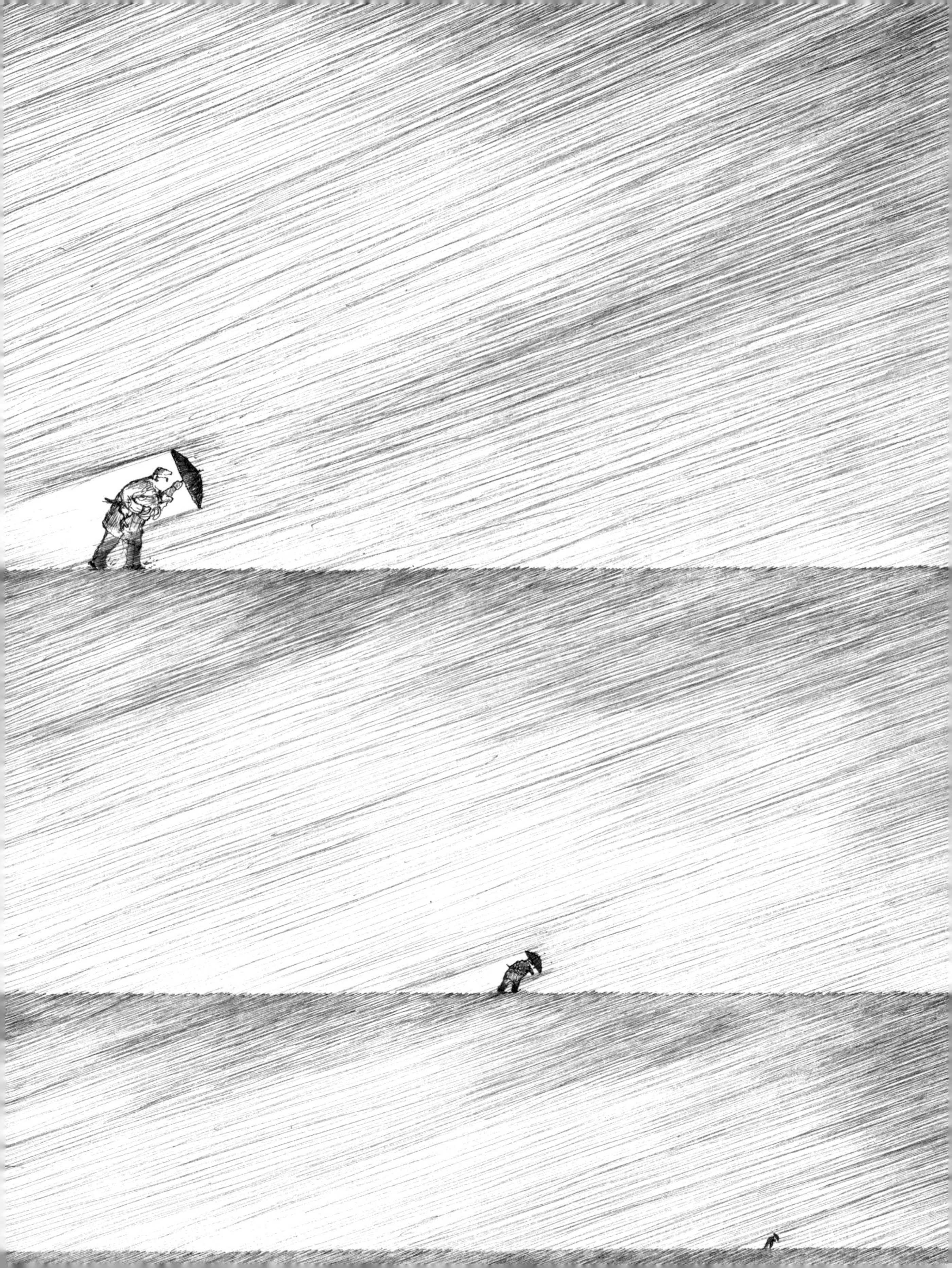

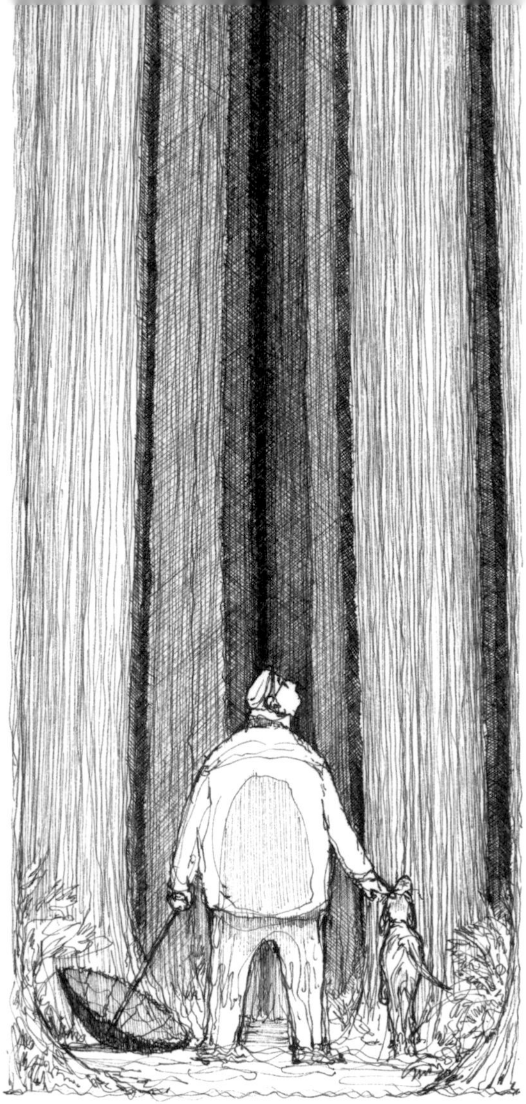

We marvelled at nature
and drew comfort from trees
that had weathered storms
for decades and still stood
strong; their endurance
reassured us.

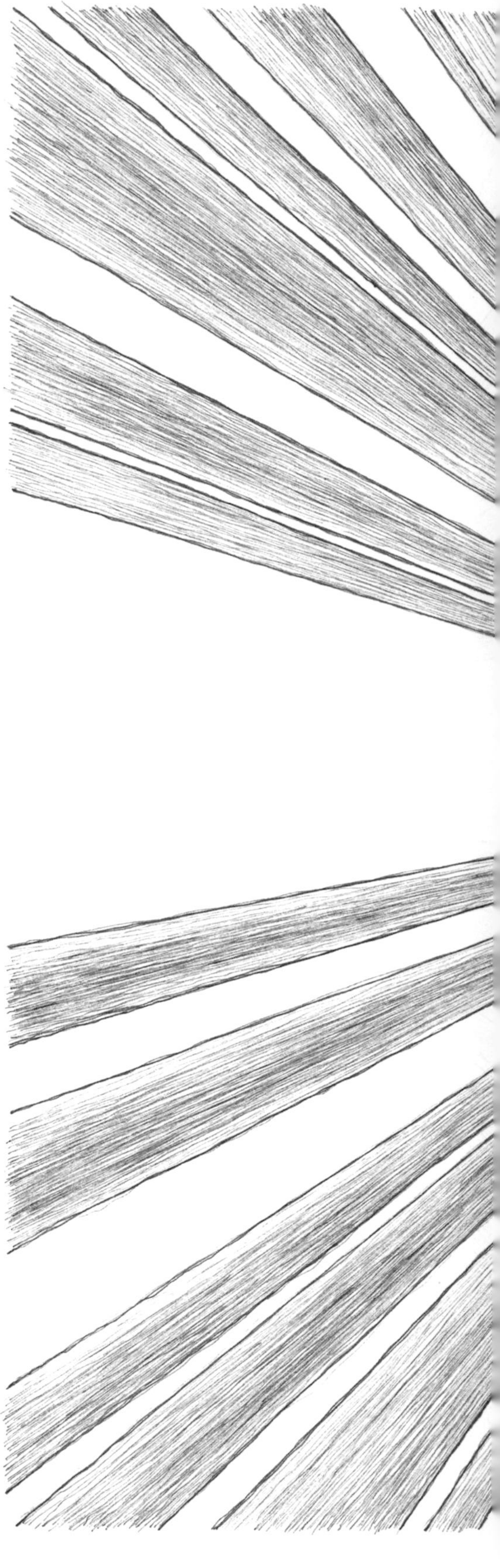

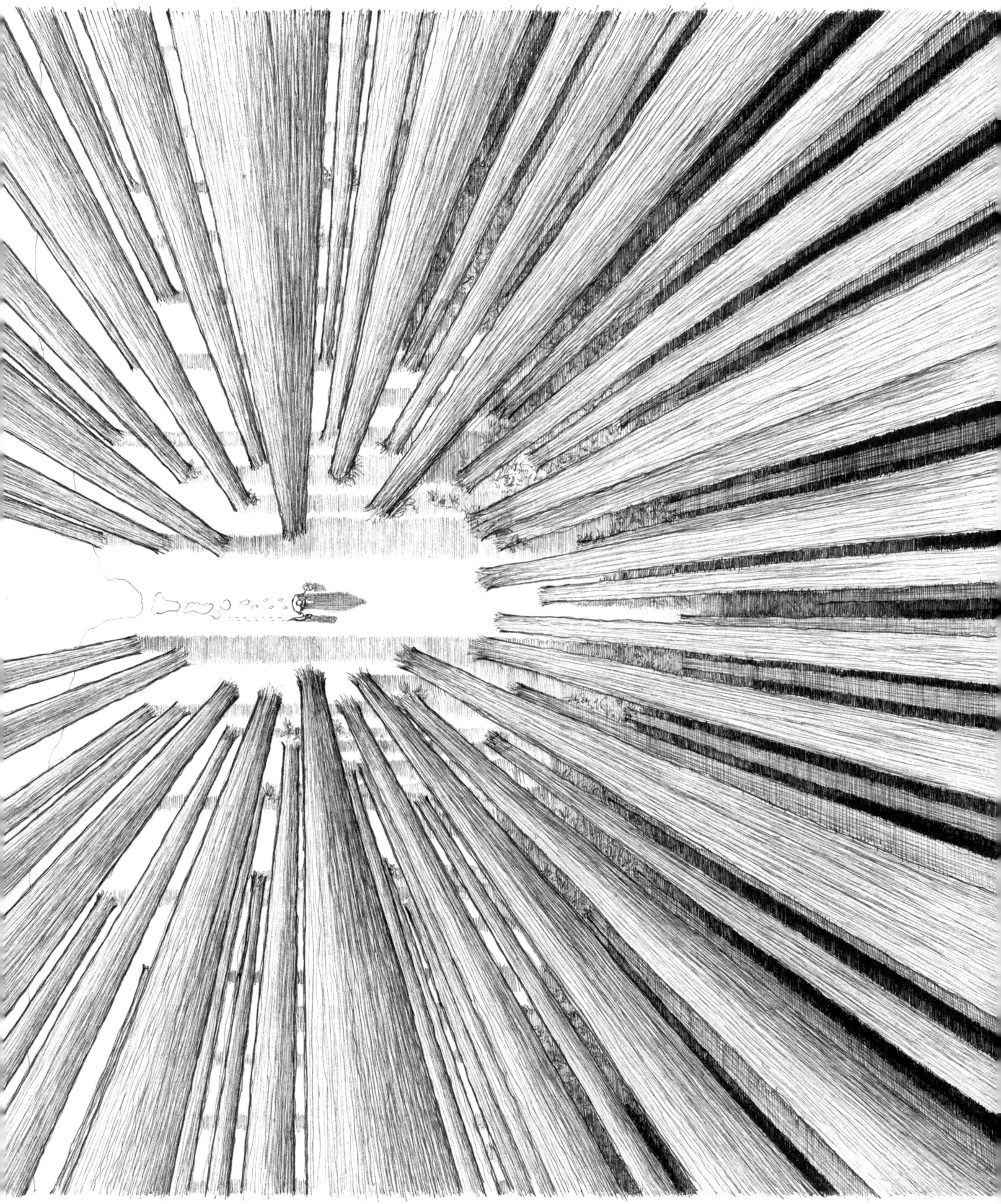

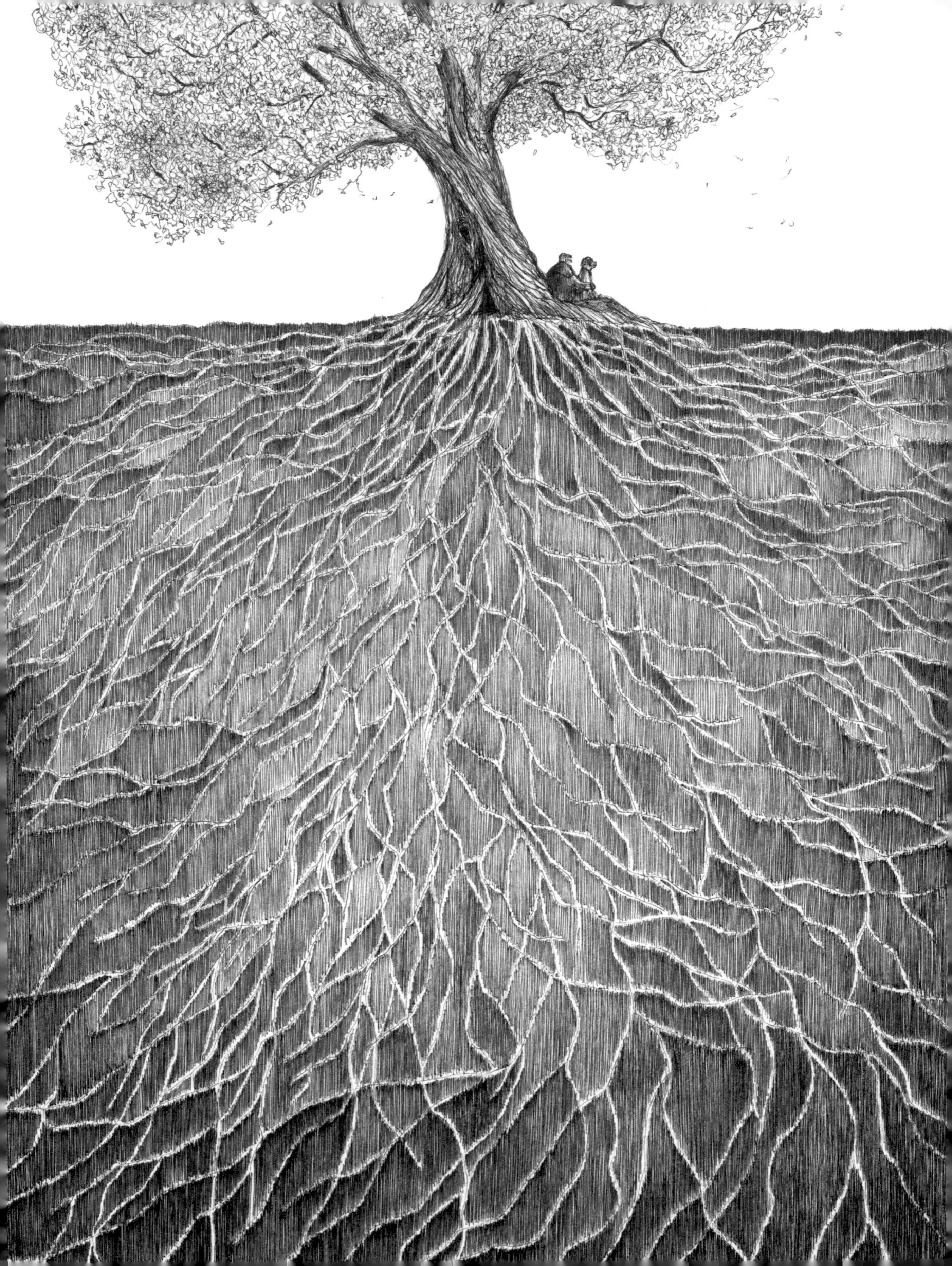

We thought about their roots, strong and silent in the earth,
and felt grounded.

In a time of uncertainty, we found comfort in the seasons.

The moon, the stars,
and the birds in the trees
watched over us.

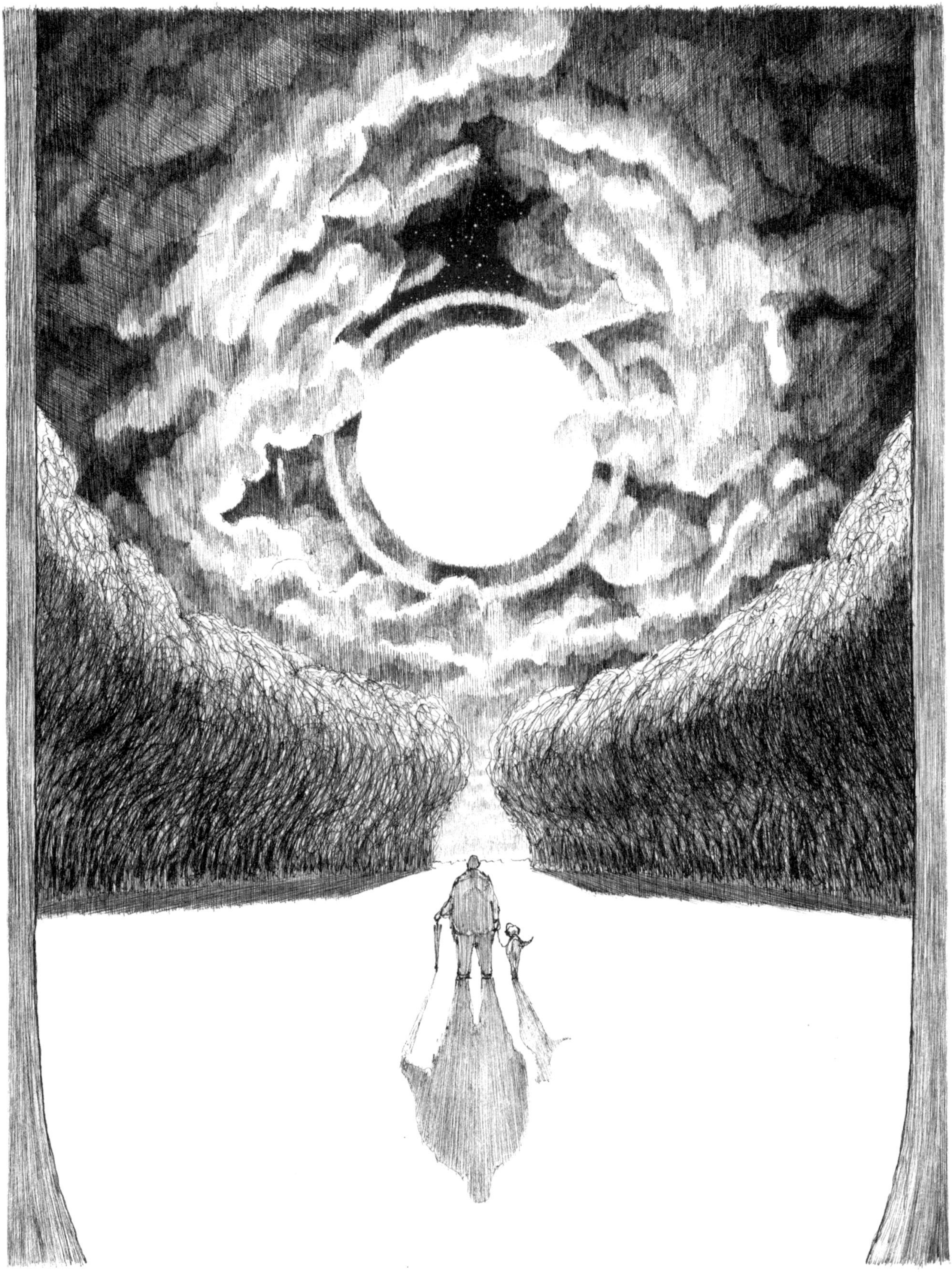

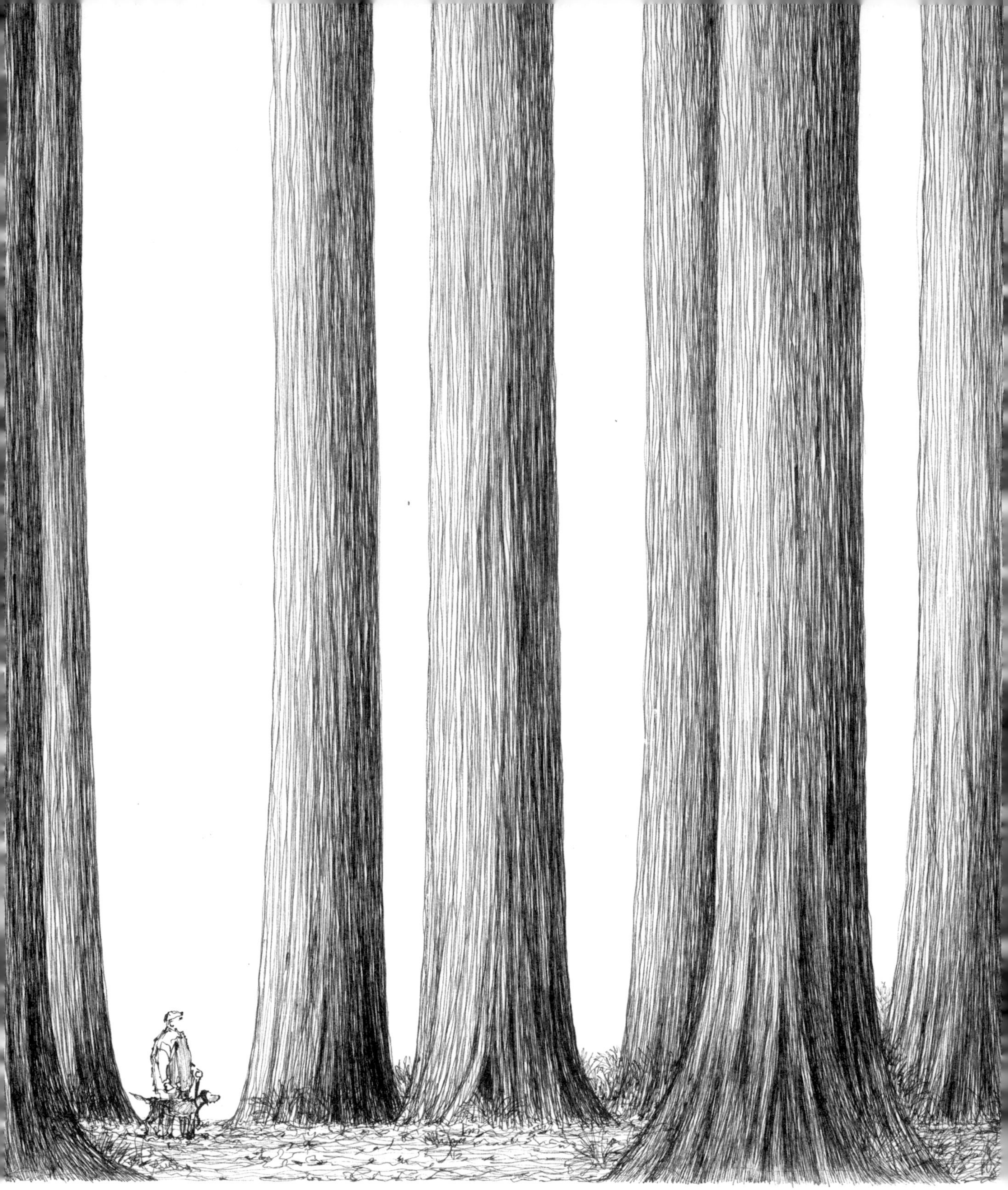

In stepping back, we had left the path clear for nature to step forwards.

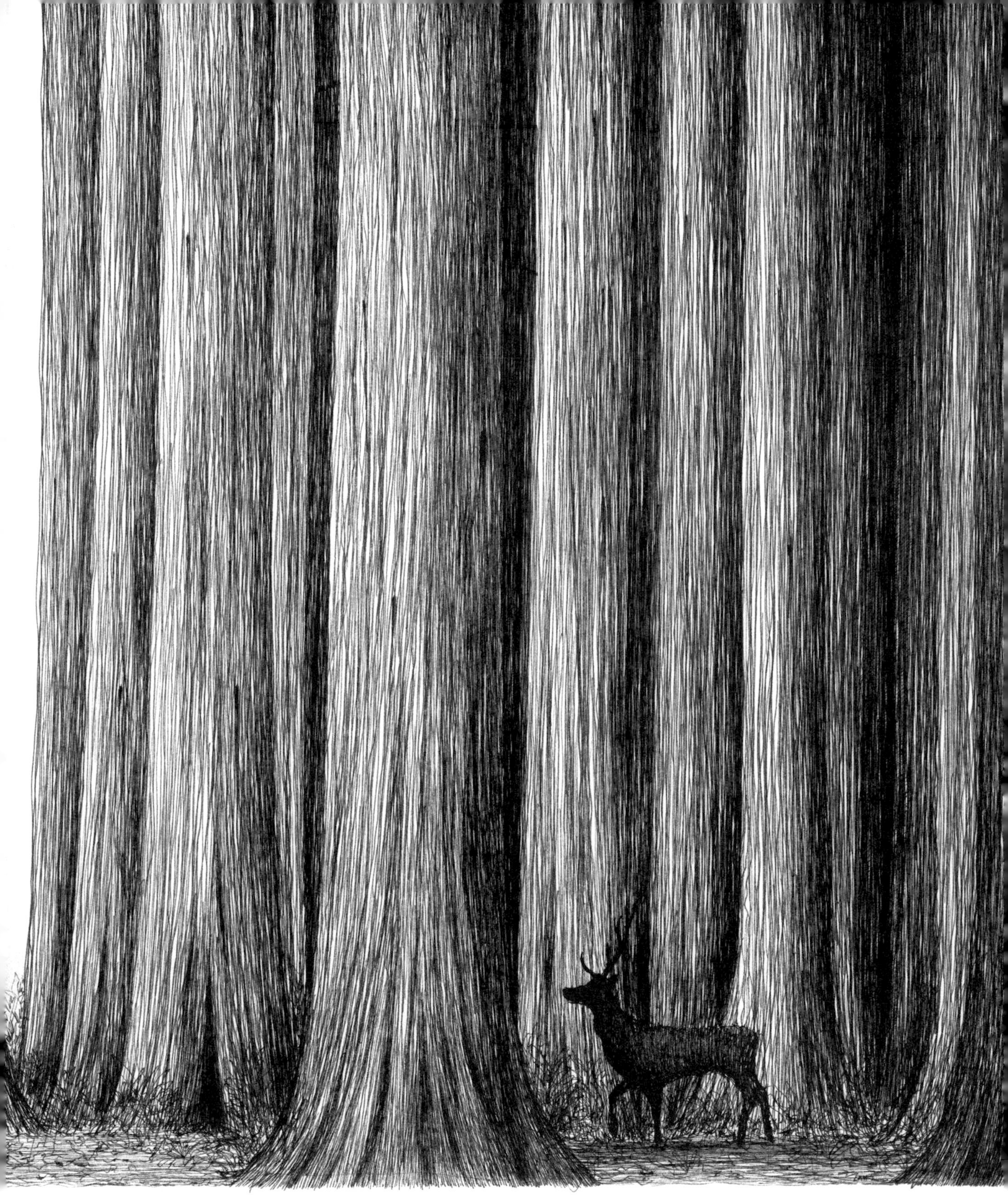

And when, slowly, the rain and winds began to subside;

when the clouds became lighter,

and at long last sunlight filtered through...

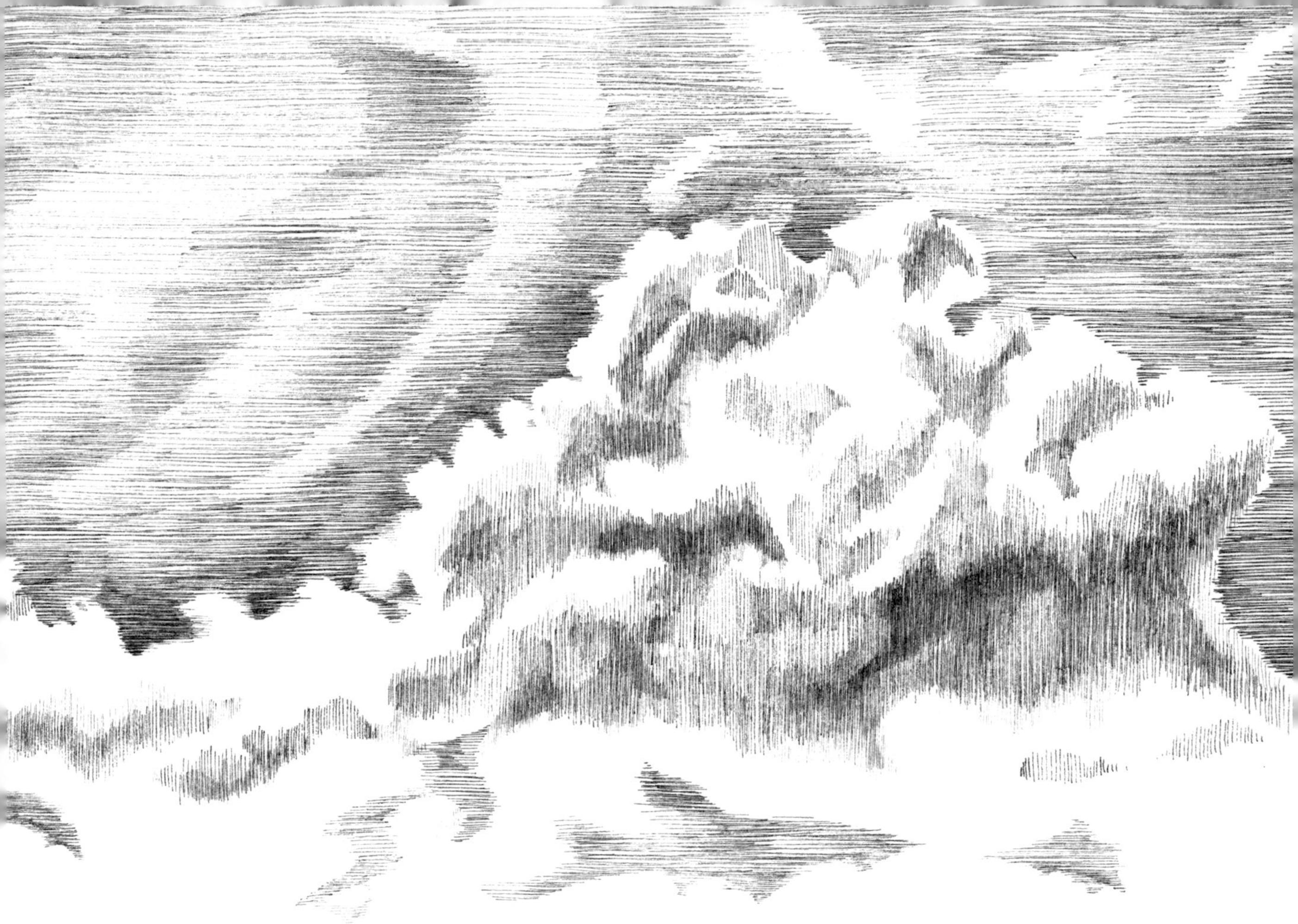

a new calm emerged.

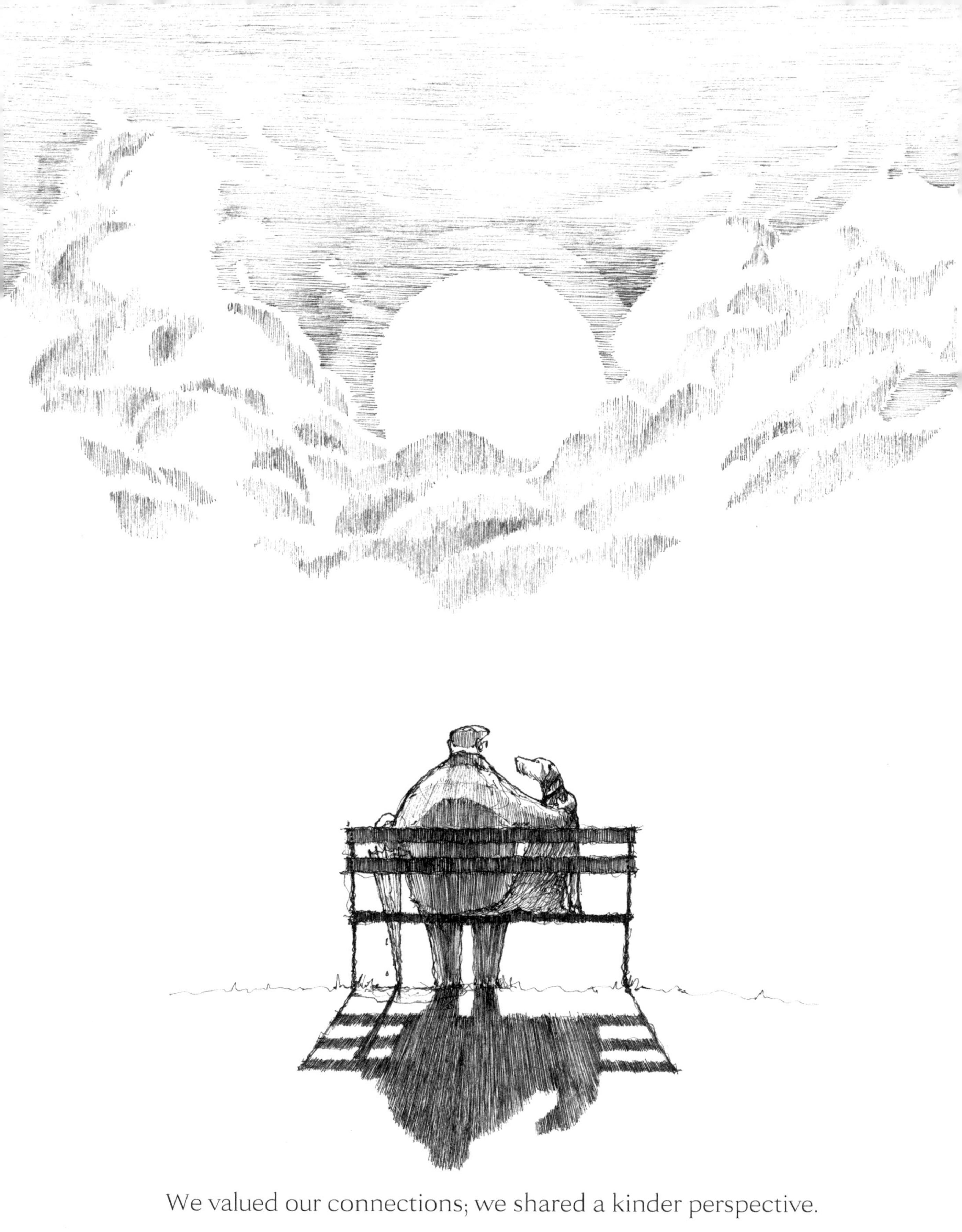

We valued our connections; we shared a kinder perspective.

And now...

we look, with hope, to the future.
Though clouds may gather again,
and we may see other storms,

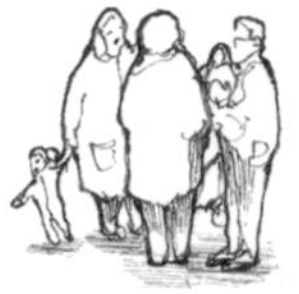

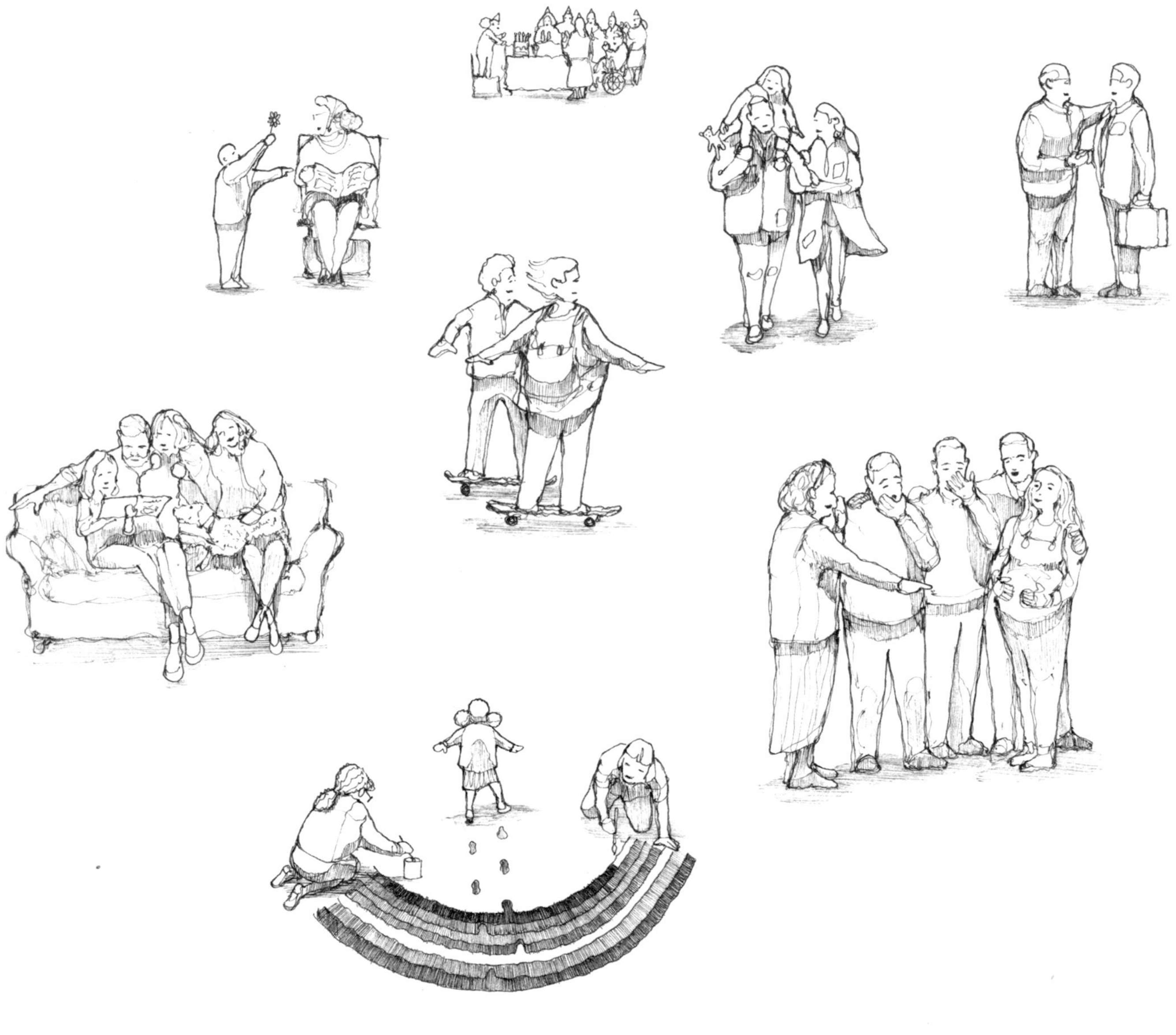

we have realised, most of all, that we're stronger facing them...

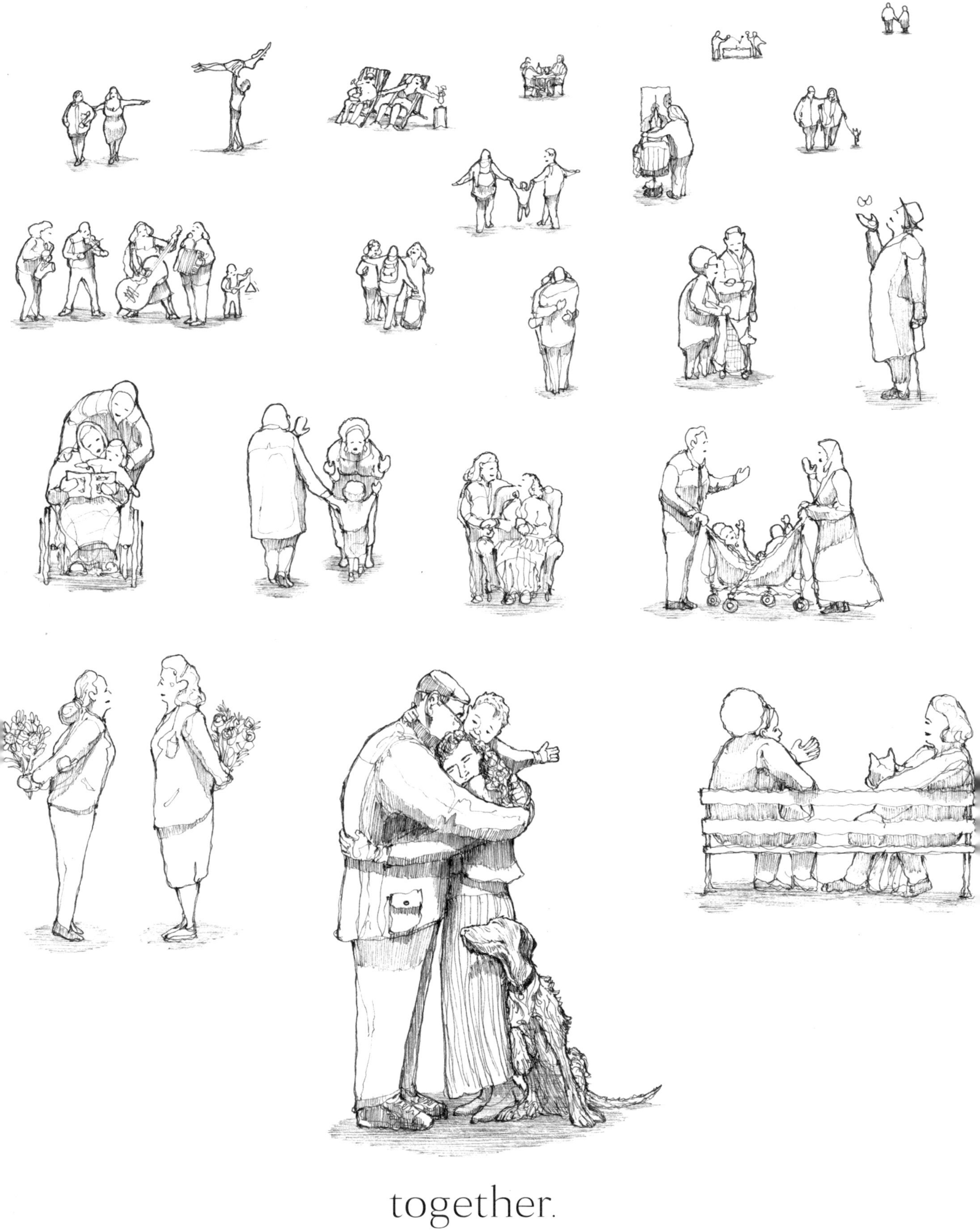

together.

Acknowledgements

This book would not have been possible without the people, places and stories that have inspired its creation.

Thank you to my grandad for becoming the main character within the book; it's been a pleasure getting to know you again.

Thank you, Lizzie: your love, support, honesty, and, most importantly, cooking make my world that much better.

To my dog, main muse and mental health coach, Robin: thanks for taking me on those much-needed walks.

Thank you to my small but perfectly formed family, who have supported me every step of the way: Mum, Harry, John, Sophie, Finlay and Bump. In fact, a special thanks is due to my mum for bringing art into my life from a young age and for the limitless praise, all those years ago, of what I now know were very questionable drawings.

Thank you to Marianne Laidlaw for finding the words to guide us through my drawings and whose belief in this book made it a reality. This book is dedicated to my grandad, and I know that Marianne, too, was thinking a lot about her much-loved Opa, Arno Geiser, while we worked on it.

Thanks to Mike Jolley for his design input and creativity.

Thanks to the team at Kyle Books for all of their hard work, especially Florence Filose for keeping everything on track, and Caroline Alberti for her production wizardry. Thanks, too, to Tara O'Sullivan for her input.

And last, but not least, a huge thank you to all those who have supported my passion for drawing over the years, both online and out and about on my travels; it means a great deal.

 @lukeadamhawker
www.lukeadamhawker.com